With every blessing
in your journey
with God

March 2011

D⊕XA

A DISCIPLESHIP COURSE

Compiled by

John B. Thomson

DARTON · LONGMAN + TODD

First published in 2007 by
Darton, Longman and Todd Ltd
1 Spencer Court
140–142 Wandsworth High Street
London SW18 4JJ

ISBN–10   0–232–52660–5
ISBN–13   978–0–232–52660–8

A catalogue record for this book is available from the British Library.

Designed and produced by Sandie Boccacci
Set in 10/12pt Times New Roman
Printed by Creative Print and Design, Wales

CONTENTS

ACKNOWLEDGEMENTS AND THANKS

DOXA is a shared project and is an attempt to display an Anglican approach to discipleship development. It therefore allows many voices to engage in conversation with each other; those of the participants, those of the contributors and those who piloted the course.

DOXA emerged as a result of my engagements with the theological ethicist, Stanley Hauerwas. It was his essay, 'The Liturgical Shape of the Christian Life: Teaching Christian Ethics as Worship',[1] which first got me thinking about this way of exploring discipleship. I am indebted to his imaginative and creative insights. I am also grateful to all the contributors to the Share Spot Resources, who embodied communal and conversational theology at its best. DOXA is an attempt to do 'common theology'; that is, theology together.

Thanks are also due to Betty Brockman, Stuart Carey, Ian Disley, Chris Gowers, Pat Holmes and Joan Robinson, who helped me develop and pilot DOXA. I am particularly grateful to groups from the following parishes in the Diocese of Sheffield: Bramley, Ecclesfield, Warmsworth, Gleadless and Millhouses, who undertook the first draft of the course and whose encouraging and sometimes critical responses helped to shape the present edition.

I am also grateful for the interest, enthusiasm and encouragement of Virginia Hearn and Brendan Walsh of Darton, Longman and Todd. Their willingness to see something special emerging out of South Yorkshire Anglicanism remains a testimony to their faith, hope and love.

Following the initial promotion of the course in the Diocese of Sheffield, I came across the work of Jeff Astley. His *Ordinary Theology: Looking, Listening and Learning in Theology*[2] helped me to appreciate the significance of what we were exploring and encouraged me to take the project further.

In particular I wish to thank those listed below for their contributions to DOXA.

Revd Robert Beard was formerly Vicar of St Peter's, Abbeydale, Sheffield.
Revd Pedr Beckley is Vicar of Greystones in Sheffield and the Bishop of Sheffield's Inform Representative.

[1] 'The Liturgical Shape of the Christian Life: Teaching Christian Ethics as Worship' in David F. Ford and Dennis L. Stamps (eds), *Essentials of Christian Community: Essays for Daniel W. Hardy* (Edinburgh: T. & T. Clark, 1996), pp. 35–48. For a fuller exposition of Stanley Hauerwas' writings see John B. Thomson, *The Ecclesiology of Stanley Hauerwas: A Christian Theology of Liberation* (Aldershot: Ashgate, 2003).

[2] Jeff Astley, *Ordinary Theology: Looking, Listening and Learning in Theology* (Aldershot: Ashgate, 2002).

8 Acknowledgements and Thanks

Revd Roger Bellamy was formerly Rector of Rawmarsh, Rotherham.

Revd David Bliss is Rector of Todwick near Sheffield and the Bishop of Sheffield's Chaplain among Deaf People.

Mr John Bouch was formerly Lay Training Officer in the Diocese of Sheffield.

Revd Patrick Coghlan is Vicar of Anston and Chair of the Partners in World Mission in the Diocese of Sheffield.

Revd Dr Ian Duffield is Vicar of St Leonard's, Sheffield and Vice Principal of the Urban Theology Unit, Sheffield.

Mrs Carmen Franklin is the Bishop of Sheffield's Adviser for Black Anglican Concerns.

Dr Christine Gore is Associate Principal of the Wilson Carlile College of Evangelism in Sheffield.

Revd Nick Helm is the Bishop of Sheffield's Adviser in Spirituality.

Revd Canon Sue Hope was formerly Missioner for the Diocese of Sheffield.

Revd Canon Nick Howe was formerly Diocesan Director of Ordinands in the Diocese of Sheffield and Chaplain to Sheffield Cathedral.

Mr Nick Hutton is the Christian Giving Adviser in the Diocese of Sheffield.

Revd Dr Emma Ineson was until recently Chaplain of Lee Abbey, Devon and curate at Dore, Sheffield.

Revd David Jeans was formerly Principal of the Wilson Carlile College of Evangelism.

Revd Nick Jowett is Vicar of St Andrews, Sharrow, Sheffield and Ecumenical Officer of the Diocese of Sheffield.

Revd George Lings is Director of the Sheffield Centre for Developing Church Planting and Evangelism in Sheffield.

Captain Ian Maher was formerly a tutor at the Wilson Carlile College of Evangelism in Sheffield.

Revd Glenn Martin is Professional Development Officer, Chaplaincy and Spiritual Healthcare, Trent Regional Health Authority and was formerly the Bishop of Sheffield's Adviser in Health and Healing.

Dr Ian McCollough was formerly the Faith in the City Development Worker for the Diocese of Sheffield.

Revd Gordon Morton was formerly a Chaplain with the Industrial Mission of South Yorkshire.

Revd Canon Martyn Percy is Principal of Ripon College Cuddesdon and Canon Theologian of Sheffield Cathedral.

Mr Malcolm Robertson was formerly Director of Education in the Diocese of Sheffield.

Revd Canon Christopher Smith is Vicar of the Minster Church of St George, Doncaster and was formerly the Bishop's Adviser in the Paranormal.

Revd Canon Gordon Taylor is Vicar of Tickhill, Doncaster.

Sr Gabrielle de Vreese is Tutor in Church History at the Wilson Carlile College of Evangelism in Sheffield.

Revd Michael Wagstaff is Social Responsibility Officer in the Diocese of Sheffield.

Revd Gary Wilton was formerly Director of Studies at the Wilson Carlile College of Evangelism in Sheffield.

Ven. John Wraw is Archdeacon of Wiltshire and formerly priest in charge of Wickersley, Rotherham, and Chair of the Diocese of Sheffield's Faith and Justice Committee.

INTRODUCTION

DOXA: God's Glory in the Ordinary

DOXA means 'glory'. As a course title this reflects the conviction that the glory of God is encountered in the ordinary experiences of life. As a child brought up during the 1960s in Uganda, East Africa, I met many 'uneducated' African Christians whose faith had a depth, commitment and wisdom which left a profound impression on me. They showed me that to be disciples is to let our lives be shaped by the mystery of God's love, mercy and grace in the midst of ordinary life. They were 'bread and butter' Christians, people who had no formal theological qualifications and yet were theologically qualified in the most important of all senses: they prayed life. Later as a vicar for eight years in inner urban Doncaster, South Yorkshire, I found a similar scenario. In a part of the country known for its low church-going were resilient Christians with a wealth of stories to tell of God's grace in their lives.

Bread and Butter Faith

As a result I believe we need to pay more attention to the faith stories of ordinary people, rather than assuming that serious reflection upon the faith is the business of academic theologians or clergy. We need to encourage them to talk about their walk. In so doing I am not being anti-intellectual or anti-academic. I am simply talking up the theological importance of the vast majority of Christians whose testimonies to the grace of God are vital if we are to appreciate the remarkable character of the God Christians worship. These testimonies generate what I am calling 'bread and butter' or 'common' theology; that is, reflections upon God's ways with life spoken by ordinary Christians as they share their stories together. It is the theology of the pew. In addition, such a focus is simply a reminder that in the ministry of Jesus those who represent the relatively powerless; the poor, the widows, the orphans, the children, the women, the unclean, are the ones God grants the privilege of revealing his glory most profoundly. Discipleship is what happens as ordinary Christian people pray through life and find themselves living as friends of Jesus Christ.

DOXA, therefore, encourages ordinary Christians to share the effects of God's work in their lives, to talk their walk. The course is about tracing holiness, that is, the way God transforms the lives of disciples. It emphasises testimony, since DOXA seeks to help people recognise how their own vision of life reflects God's work in them. This is why the sharing that happens can be called 'Testimony Theology' or 'reflection upon God at work in grass-roots Christians' lives'. In this way we hope such Christians will become more confident in their witness to God's grace in their lives.

DOXA and Public Worship

DOXA focuses upon the Eucharist because this is at the heart of most of Anglican Sunday worship. The Eucharist is where the church gathers and celebrates the Gospel dramatically. It is the ongoing sacramental sign of the grace of God. By engaging with the *practices* of Eucharistic worship, DOXA focuses upon what we are doing as we worship and what this is doing to us. Practices are the way communities exhibit, explore and develop their life. They are not about putting into practice ideas held in advance but are more like a craftswoman developing the practical wisdom of weaving. Practical wisdom emerges in and through practising the craft. The Greeks used the word *phronesis* to distinguish this sort of wisdom from that of the scholar, which they called *sophia*. DOXA therefore seeks to avoid any sense that discipleship is simply a package of ideas. Discipleship is what we do as we live open to God; it is our walk with the Lord. Meeting to worship, therefore, is like joining a training session. The practices of the Eucharist, such as gathering to worship, confession, listening to Scripture, receiving the sacraments etc. craft Christians into mature disciples since they train us in how to live with God. In short, discipleship is developed through the communal training of public worship, training which is put to the test in daily life.

This attention to the craft of Christian discipleship and to the witness of ordinary Christians is particularly important today when the institutional church is under criticism both from without and from within. Criticism from without tends to focus upon supposedly authoritarian and manipulative tendencies within organised religion. Criticism from within tends to focus upon the need for a simpler, sharper and tidier faith, which can market itself in the public square to get a hearing. Both imply that human initiative can control or determine God's activity. DOXA, in contrast, seeks to explore what God is doing in ordinary Christians' lives as course participants are invited to share their understanding of discipleship as it is patterned by their worship and tested in their daily lives. Discipleship is developed as Christians pay attention to, listen to and gaze upon God. DOXA assumes that God will transform those who are open to his grace and that the stories such disciples tell will indicate the character of the God doing the transforming.

Such transformation includes becoming increasingly aware of the wisdom present in the wider Christian community. So to supplement and enrich the insights of participants we have included a Share Spot in each session. The Share Spots and the thoughts shared in the Share Spot resources sections are opportunities to listen to how fellow disciples understand their faith; how they talk their walk. They are not

the final word on the theme, nor are they exhaustive accounts. Rather they are contributions to the conversations taking place within the group. Participants are
encouraged to read the resources section before each session in order to be able to
engage with this material during the group time.

DOXA, therefore, is not about teaching the liturgy so much as disclosing how the
liturgy opens Christians up to God's transforming grace. As such those who have
been Christians for some time will find their understanding of the Eucharist
enriched and appreciate more fully the way participating in worship nourishes their
discipleship. In addition those new to the faith can begin to recognise the shape of
Christian living as they begin to recognise how the liturgy trains Christians for life
with God today. This approach is also open-ended since the wisdom that emerges as
ordinary Christians reflect upon their worship practices is ongoing. We all have
more to learn. It is a bit like learning a language. We learn how to speak by practising with other speakers rather than needing to be taught by professors. Professors
help us to understand the language more richly by enabling us to appreciate the form
of the language and how the language has been spoken or written by others.
Similarly scholarly and clerical theological wisdom serves the church by assisting
ordinary Christians to locate their own discipleship dialects within the wider
Christian language. It does not replace those dialects.

DOXA encourages conversations between different disciples as they reflect upon
their conversation with God embodied in their worship together. Like all conversations, detailed outcomes are not guaranteed in advance. There is an openness about
conversations and thus an element of surprise involved. As such we believe it
represents an attractive way of enriching discipleship at a time when many inside
and beyond the institutional church are hostile to forms of control and closure by the
powerful. In contrast to approaches which seek to tell people what to believe or
which give the impression of possessing all the answers to faith questions in
advance, DOXA presumes that faith is a relational and lifelong journey rather than
a fixed ideology. Hence the wisdom of God is constantly being discovered and
developed, and fresh insights are emerging as God transforms his people.

DOXA also has an evangelistic dimension. Worship is evangelistic in the sense
that God-with-us is always the Gospel, the good news. Indeed, as a vicar for eight
years in Doncaster, I found that the congregation grew precisely because worship
evangelised.[3] The sense of encounter with God and the hospitality of the community which gathered to worship meant that newcomers stayed. So exploring what God
is doing among us as we worship illuminates further the character and transforming
power of the Gospel. God refuses to be absent from those gathering in his name.
Likewise, DOXA restores the link between belonging and believing. Belonging

---

[3] See John B. Thomson, *Church on Edge? Practising Christian Ministry Today* (London: Darton,
Longman and Todd, 2004).

actively to church is seen to be vital to ongoing discipleship development, since worship shapes our discipleship. We are, after all, participating consciously in God and being divinised or transformed to share in God's life forever. As this happens, others see the difference Christ makes in the world and in our lives.

DOXA and Discipleship

DOXA does not begin with an abstract idea called 'discipleship' which it tries to convince participants about. DOXA assumes that those taking the course are already disciples since otherwise they would not be part of the course. They are already walking with God. So DOXA begins with the people who gather to reflect together and says, 'Here are people who sense that Christ is at work in their lives and are willing to reflect upon and share what this means to them.' Discipleship is described by their lives because God is inscribed in their lives. Of course discipleship is also about what God has been doing in other people's lives, past and present, and the Share Spots are a way of contributing to the understanding of discipleship present in the group. However, the intention of DOXA is that a richer understanding of Christian discipleship emerges through the conversations within the group rather than being defined abstractly. Thus the distinctive discipleship of participants will be revealed through the course. It may therefore be helpful, at the beginning of the course or section of the course undertaken, to have a brief discussion about participants' understanding of their discipleship. A richer discussion will be had at the conclusion of the time together, when the group has listened to each other's discipleship reflections and engaged with the Share Spot material. Such a discussion might well take place during a group Eucharist at the end of the course.

DOXA and other Christian traditions

DOXA has been developed in an English Anglican context and reflects this distinctive Christian dialect. It is possible to use the liturgy of other Christian traditions in place of Common Worship, although the 'fit' may not be as easy. In addition, some of the Share Spot material would need to be contrasted with other Christian traditions' practices or understandings. This might involve more liaison with the ministers of those traditions. However, as a spin-off, this might enable DOXA to inform other traditions of Anglican self-understanding and, particularly in a mixed church group, could encourage lively discussion. Certainly DOXA is not suggesting that Anglicans have got it all right. Rather it is enabling Anglicans and non-Anglicans to share in such a way that both gain a deeper understanding of discipleship in the Anglican stream. In this way Christian unity is actually helped, since distinctive Christian pedigrees are not ignored or colonised, but rather offered for mutual illumination.

DOXA Summary

DOXA is different because:

- it explores how worship trains disciples.
- it explores the effects of practising Christianity.
- it explores testimony theology.
- It allows people's lives to illuminate discipleship.
- it is rooted in Anglican worship but can be adapted for other traditions.
- it is aimed at those who have some experience of Christian worship.
- it is about listening to how God is shaping ordinary Christian lives in and through worship; that is, 'common theology'.

What's in a name?
As we have seen earlier, DOXA means 'glory'. For Christians:

- God is always 'God-with-us', Immanuel.
- the human condition is one saturated and upheld by God-with-us as Holy Spirit.
- worship involves apprehending God's glory in our ordinariness.
- worship involves gazing upon the glory of God and thereby discovering the language and dialects of Christian believing.

Why this approach and who's it for?
DOXA began life as a discipleship course developed for the Diocese of Sheffield. Our aim was:

- to focus upon ordinary Christian disciples.
- to develop a different style of course from others on offer.
- to offer a course which would be able to engage all traditions within the diocese.
- to enable congregations to begin from where they were and explore faith initially from within the traditions they represented.
- to offer a flexible course which could be used in different ways according to local need.

As a result *Common Worship* emerged as a 'common' and constructive place to begin. In Anglican thinking *Common Worship*:

- is where the glory of God is publicly attended to.
- is where the glory of God-with-us forms those who worship into a holy people.
- is how we gather to celebrate our participation in the glory of God.
- is the occasion where the church as a whole, laity and clergy together, seek to listen for God.

We hope that this course will continue to engage Christians of all traditions in this spirit.

What's DOXA about?

DOXA is rooted in a way of listening for God often expressed in the phrase *lex orandi, lex credendi* ('the law of prayer as the law of believing' or 'what we pray indicates what we believe'). For Anglicans in particular, listening for God involves:

- attending to the interplay of Scripture, tradition and sound learning (reason) as these are webbed together in the experience of public common worship.
- public prayer. Prayer is never private, even if it can be solitary. Prayer is always a participation with others in the offering of life to God in Jesus Christ.
- liturgical listening. Liturgy, from the Greek *leitourgia* meaning 'public service', is the way public prayer is configured so that our personal praying is always anchored in the wisdom of the wider Christian community.
- participation. Common worship reminds us that listening for God properly requires everybody's participation and sharing of wisdom, since otherwise our hearing will be inadequate.

DOXA Facilitator's Notes

DOXA:

- is an *18 week course* inviting ordinary Christians to reflect upon what God is doing to them as they worship together.
- is flexible and can be done as a *whole or in parts*, e.g., as an Advent series or a Lent series using a section or two at a time.
- is best done in *groups* of between 6–10.
- needs a *group facilitator* and a *host*.
- needs a *well heated/ventilated room* with *comfortable seating*. It is important to ensure that the atmosphere puts people at their ease, whether the gathering is in a public room or in a home. Having refreshments available as people arrive and halfway through the session is helpful. The host looks after this, allowing the facilitator to concentrate on the course.
- needs *facilitating* rather than leading. *Facilitating* is not about teaching people or ensuring they keep on message. It is about enabling people to share their stories and to listen to each other's insights. Thus it is important that facilitators do not try to control the content of the discussion but let people have their say. For example, if a discussion is proving productive, there is no need to keep rigidly to the structure. Equally it is not essential that every question is used. The facilitator can decide to ignore some questions if the discussion is flowing and time is pressing. What is important is that people share and listen to each other's faith. A facilitator, however, will need to ensure that no-one dominates the group or is inhibited from contributing. Unless all participate, the exercise will be inadequate.

DOXA has 6 sections of 3 × 1.5 hours:

- each session has *prayer time.*
- each has reflection upon a *liturgical practice.*[4]
- each engages with a *Bible passage.*
- each has a *challenge task* to work on something further and bring back to the next session.
- each includes a *Share Spot* with resources provided. The resource material does not consist of expert opinions, but the wisdom of trusted folk on the Christian journey. The idea is that participants read them and decide how they illuminate the themes being shared in the group.
- each has a *Ponder Point*, which invites participants to reflect upon their deepening understanding of discipleship.

---

[4] Liturgical quotations are from *Common Worship: Services and Prayers for the Church of England*. © The Archbishop's Council of the Church of England.

DOXA Facilitator's Preparation

- Pray for the group and ensure you know people's names.
- Make sure there are enough copies of the course for each participant.
- Give copies of the course to participants before the first session so that they can prepare.
- Encourage participants to bring a Bible with them.
- Read the session material, including the Share Spot resources, beforehand, and ensure that any extra materials needed are provided.
- Prepare using the suggested timings but be ready to be flexible when you feel that the group needs this. End on time.
- Think about how you will help people to listen to each other, particularly when they may not agree.
- Encourage participants to get a notebook to record insights and responses to the challenge sections.
- Ensure that refreshments are arranged with the host and timings are clear.
- Your job is not to give people the 'right answers' but to ensure that people can share their own responses to worship. It doesn't matter if you are not sure of everything since you are not there to teach the group the faith. However if you do find something that perplexes the group, note it, get in touch with your minister/priest and report back to the group on the next occasion.
- Decide with the group in the first session whether you want to do the Seder Meal in Section E, Session 2: Memory and Meals. A Seder Meal pack (price in 2005 £7.50) can be ordered from CMJ, Olive Press, 30c Clarence Road, St. Albans, AL1 4JJ, email: enquiries@cmj.org.uk, website: www.cmj.org.uk. It may be worth suggesting that the church or church district/diocese gets a pack which the group borrows.

DOXA Host's Preparation

- Ensure the room is warm, well lit and the seating comfortable.
- Ensure participants can see each other.
- Provide refreshments upon arrival and halfway through the session.
- Ensure participants know where the toilets are, especially if the meeting is in a public room rather than a home.
- If the meeting is in a public room, ensure that health and safety information is shared with the group.

DOXA: Course Outline

Section A: Gathering and Greeting

Session 1: Worship as Community
Share Spot Resources:
- Worship and Discipleship: John Thomson
- Worship and Ecumenism: Nick Jowett
- Worship and Church Buildings: Roger Bellamy

Session 2: Worship as Celebration
Share Spot Resources:
- Worship and Other Faiths: Robert Beard
- Parish and Worship: John Thomson

Session 2: Worship as Service
Share Spot Resources:
- Vocation and Discipleship: John Thomson
- Vocation and Work: Gordon Morton
- Vocation: Lay Ministry: John Bouch
- Vocation: Ordination: Nick Howe

Section B: Penitence and Prayer

Session 1: Lamenting Life
Share Spot Resources:
- Penitential Practices in the Church of England: Roger Bellamy
- Theodicy: God and Suffering: David Jeans

Session 2: Dealing with Damage
Share Spot Resources:
- Church and Healing: Glenn Martin
- The Church and the Paranormal: Christopher Smith

Session 3: A Praying People
Share Spot Resources:
- Ways of Prayer: Nick Helm
- Problems in Prayer: Nick Helm

Section C: The Liturgy of the Word

Session 1: The Bible as Hearing Aid
Share Spot Resources:
- Lectionary Reading: John Thomson
- The Bible in England: Christine Gore
- The Divine Drama: Christine Gore

Session 2: Bible Reading
Share Spot Resources:
- Ways of Reading and Studying the Bible: Ian Duffield
- Scripture and Anglicanism: John Thomson

Session 3: Sharing the Word of the Lord
Share Spot Resources:
- Imaginative Preaching: John Thomson
- Worship and Doctrine: David Jeans

Section D: The Liturgy of the Sacraments: Baptism

Session 1: Gaining Access
Share Spot Resources:
- Baptism: Emma Ineson

Session 2: Travelling Together
Share Spot Resources:
- Sacraments: John Thomson

Session 3: 'Yes, Minister!'
Share Spot Resources:
- Discipleship, Strangers and the Image of God: Ian McCollough
- Ministry and Synods: Gordon Taylor

Section E: The Liturgy of the Sacraments: The Eucharist

Session 1: Thanksgiving
Share Spot Resources:
- Christian Giving: Nick Hutton

• Christianity and Regeneration: Michael Wagstaff

Session 2: Memory and Meals
Share Spot Resources:
• The Eucharist: Emma Ineson

Session 3: Community and Creation
Share Spot Resources:
• Christianity and Disability: David Bliss
• Christianity and Development: John Thomson
• Christianity and Gender: John Thomson
• Christianity and Industry: Gordon Morton
• Christianity and Race: Carmen Franklin
• Christianity, Urban Life and the Mission Journey: Ian McCollough

Section F: Sending Forth

Session 1: Mission and the Holy Spirit
Share Spot Resources:
• The Holy Spirit and Mission: Sue Hope
• The History of Christian Mission: Gabrielle de Vreese
• Church Planting Today: George Lings

Session 2: Mission and the Good News
Share Spot Resources:
• Evangelism Today: Gary Wilton
• The Gospel in Society: Ian Maher
• The Church and Cults: Pedr Beckley
• Mission and the Overseas Church: Patrick Coghlan

Session 3: Mission and Service
Share Spot Resources:
• Love of God, Love of Neighbour: John Wraw
• Parish Evangelism: John Thomson
• Mission and Education: Malcolm Robertson

GATHERING AND GREETING

WORSHIP AS COMMUNITY

Welcome and Prayer (5mins)

Introduction (15mins)

In this first session we are 'gathering together'. In pairs, spend a minute giving each other a potted story of your life. As a group, let each person spend 30 seconds introducing their partner to other group members.

• How much do you know of each other?

As we go through this course, it is essential that we recognise the mystery of one another and respect how different we are. Listening to one another and confidentiality are therefore vital to the success of the group.

It is also important that our own self-learning is recognised. Throughout this course you may wish to keep a journal recording what you are learning as you go along.

Aim of This Session
To explore what gathering to worship means.

Liturgy
The Gathering
The Lord be with you
and also with you.

Reflection (20mins)

Picture yourself in church on a Sunday at the Eucharist.

• What does the 'gathering and greeting' suggest about the God you worship and the church you worship with?
• What does the greeting 'the Lord be with you' mean to you?
• Share what this prayer says to you about discipleship.

Picture the church building and, if you have one, the graveyard.

• What do they say about Christian worship and people's lives and deaths?

Bible Bit (20mins)

2 Corinthians 5:16–19
(This passage comes at a point in the letter when St Paul is pleading with the fractious Corinthian church to see their life together in the light of Christ.)

• How does this passage shed light upon what you've been sharing?
• How does this passage invite you to regard your congregation and yourself?
• How does worshipping together shape your view of each other?

Share Spot (15mins)

Talk about the Share Spot resources for this session, which explore further insights into worship as community.

• How does worship shape discipleship?
• Ecumenism is when churches seek to come closer together. How might worship aid this?
• In what way can church buildings aid or inhibit worship today?

Ponder Point (5mins)

What has this session clarified about your discipleship?

Challenge

• Find time this week to record what you have learned from this session.
• For the next session, draw a pathway of your life, marking significant moments on it. Think how your being part of the church has contributed to its shape.
• Prepare for the next meeting by going through the next session.

Share Spot Resources

Worship and Discipleship
JOHN THOMSON

ROOTS
Worship, historically, appears to be inspired by awe and lament; awe in the face of the grandeur of life and the universe; lament in response to the tragedy of suffering,

finitude and death. Worship reflects the conviction that life is a gift. Hence worship involves delight, thanks, glory, celebration, trust and hope. In the Jewish-Christian traditions, especially, it is more than response and is certainly not wishful thinking. Rather, it is about transformation. As individuals worship, God transforms them into a people whose lives speak of God's presence in the world. Discipleship is the out-working of this in daily living. Worship, therefore, is about paying attention to the God whom Christians believe is both beyond us (transcendent) and yet intimate (immanent). It necessarily involves ritual and story; ritual as a shared way of patterning life; story as a way of integrating life within an ongoing narrative of God's ways with creation.

THE OLD TESTAMENT
Worship fills the Old Testament. Walter Brueggemann makes the distinction between Festival Praise (celebrations such as the Passover, the Festival of Weeks and the Feast of Tabernacles [Exodus 23:14–16]), Prophetic Praise (the interpretation of worship's challenges for the day) and Exilic Praise (remembrance: the writing down of holy history when Israel were in exile). The Psalms, in particular, are theology as praise. Throughout, a distinctive connection is made between worship and ethics, liturgy and life. Furthermore, it was the Old Testament which first grasped the oneness of God (monotheism).

JUDAISM
Following the destruction of the temple in 586 BC, Judaism's worship was increasingly focused around synagogues and the practical obedience of the Torah or written revelation of God with its interpretation by the rabbis (the Mishnah and the Talmud). Later the Pharisees sought to give practical expression to Jewish popular piety. Public prayer, devotion and discipleship were especially important as a witness to imperial overlords.

THE NEW TESTAMENT
Jesus' life and teaching embodied life lived with God as Father. The Lord's Prayer is Jesus' worship shared with his disciples. For St Matthew, Jesus replaces the yoke of the Torah (Matthew 11:28–30), whilst for St Paul, Jesus extends the availability of God in worship to all people, Jew or Gentile. Jesus' ministry is about sharing blessing, yet the cross includes the tragic within the triumph of the worship of God. Jesus' companions are those who know the grace of God's love, forgiveness and indestructible life in their own lives and live within this horizon. Christian worship is therefore necessarily corporate and involves learning discipleship through participating in shared worship.

THE CHURCH

The worship of the church celebrates the transforming grace of God in Jesus Christ experienced at different times and in different places. There is therefore no single way of worshipping. However, over time within the Christian community some basic agreements about the character of God and the limits of acceptable expressions of worship have emerged. Hence by the fourth century AD God was worshipped as Trinity (Father, Son and Spirit). Equally from the earliest times, the shape of public worship has included the reading of Scripture, confession, creed and prayers. For Anglicans this is expressed in the notion of Common Worship; common in the sense that it is agreed upon by the whole community, in England represented in the General Synod and Parliament, yet sufficiently flexible so that the particularities of time, place and cultures can be respected.

CONCLUSION

Worship therefore exposes people to God, the source of life, and trains Christians in their discipleship. It represents an ecology of praise, a symphony of gratitude to God for the gift of life and a protest against human arrogance. It connects memory, reflection, imagination and expectation as it looks forward to that great celebration of glory which we call heaven. It trains Christians to be faithful witnesses to the grace of God in ordinary living.

BOOKS, ETC.

Breen, Mike and Kallestad, Walt, *The Passionate Church: The Art of Life-Changing Discipleship* (Eastbourne: Kingsway, 2005)

Brown, David, *Discipleship and Imagination: Christian Tradition and Truth* (Oxford: OUP, 2000)

Brueggemann, Walter, *Israel's Praise: Doxology Against Idolatry and Ideology* (Philadelphia: Fortress Press, 1988)

—*Theology of the Old Testament: Testimony, Dispute, Advocacy* (Minneapolis: Fortress Press, 1997)

Earey, Mark, *Liturgical Worship: A fresh look, how it works, why it matters* (London: Church House Publishing, 2002)

Hardy, Daniel W. and Ford, David F., *Jubilate: Theology in Praise* (London: Darton, Longman and Todd, 1984)

Jones, Cheslyn, Wainwright, Geoffrey, Yarnold, Edward, and Bradshaw, Paul, *The Study of Liturgy* (London: SPCK, 1992)

Perham, Michael, *Celebrate the Christian Story: An Introduction to the New Lectionary and Calendar* (London: SPCK, 1997)

Thomson, John B., *Church on Edge? Practising Christian Ministry Today* (London: Darton, Longman and Todd, 2004)

Wells, Samuel, *Improvisation: The Drama of Christian Ethics* (London: SPCK, 2004)

Wright, Tom, *Following Jesus: Biblical Reflections on Discipleship* (London: SPCK, 1998)

Worship and Ecumenism
NICK JOWETT

The Church's worship has changed and developed throughout twenty centuries. From the simple and spontaneous 'breaking of the Word' and sharing in the love feast in houses in the first century to the formalities of a splendid medieval cathedral High Mass is a huge leap. And when in history the Church has split and divided, this has usually involved conflict about worship and has resulted in great changes in worship. The Eastern (Orthodox) Church split from the Western (Roman Catholic) Church in the eleventh century; as a very broad generalisation one can say that the Eastern Church has always been more conservative in retaining ancient forms of worship, and even into the twenty-first century Orthodox Christians continue to doubt the validity of modern ecumenical worship. The Protestant Reformation of the sixteenth century eventually produced many different denominations (e.g. Lutheran, Calvinist/Reformed, Anglican, Baptist) which moved away from control by Rome and adopted very different worship styles (use of local language instead of Latin, rejection of ceremonies and images, a strong focus on the Bible and preaching, denial of the Mass as some kind of repeated sacrifice of Christ or as an automatic bearer of merit). The Protestant world has continued to give birth to new denominations (e.g. Methodism, Pentecostalism), each with its own styles and traditions of worship.

This has resulted in some fundamental oppositions in worship:

'LITURGICAL' OR 'FREE'?
Anglican worship has followed Catholic tradition in making use of authorised written liturgies. Many but not all Protestant denominations have preferred a more spontaneous, Spirit-led style of worship, with no fixed forms, the congregation using only a hymnbook, if anything.

'WORD' OR 'TABLE'?
The architecture and arrangement of a church building often give away the emphasis and focal point of worship. Enter many a Methodist church and you will find a large central pulpit; go into the typical cruciform parish church and your eye will be led up to the altar at the east end. This tells you that the one church values the preaching of the Word most highly, the other emphasises the sacrament of Holy Communion as the heart of the church's life. On the Catholic-Protestant spectrum, those at the Protestant end will value the Word, those at the Catholic end the sacrament, more highly.

'SACRIFICE' OR 'MEMORIAL'?
There is a wide spectrum in the way different churches (and different Christians

within churches) understand the Eucharist: at the Catholic end of the spectrum Christ is substantially present in the bread and wine and the action of the Eucharist effectively re-presents what Christ achieved on Calvary; at the Protestant end of the spectrum the Eucharist is a simple memorial meal.

'WORDS' OR 'SILENCE'?
Much worship, both Catholic and Protestant, is full of words, read, sung, proclaimed. By contrast, the Quakers sit in silence, waiting for the Spirit of God to speak within them; they may choose to share that with others present, or not.

'ICONS' OR 'SIMPLICITY'?
Partly because of its Jewish heritage ('You shall not make for yourselves an idol ... nor bow down to them'), there has often been anxiety among some Christians about the use of images in worship. Eastern Orthodox Christians awaken in themselves the reality and wonder of the incarnation by venerating icons. At different times, by contrast, some Orthodox Christians in the east and Puritan Christians in the west have destroyed much Christian art in churches because it seemed to them idolatry, removing the mind and heart from pure spiritual worship.

Many other polar opposites of Christian worship could be mentioned. The scandal of disunity, however, began to make a serious impact on the minds and hearts of Christians about one hundred years ago, and the twentieth century saw increasingly effective attempts to bring the different churches back into dialogue, reconciliation, covenant relationships, collaboration and in some cases reunion. Among the achievements of the ecumenical movement in relation to worship are:

• The rediscovery by many churches in the Western tradition (thanks also to the Liturgical Movement) of the fundamental shape of the Eucharist, going back to the earliest Christian centuries. Go into a Methodist or a United Reformed or an Anglican or a Catholic Eucharist today, and you will find more similarities than differences.
• 'Free' churches have discovered the value of well-written liturgies; liturgical churches have discovered the excitement of spontaneity within fixed structures.
• Eucharistic mutual hospitality is now a fact between many denominations. (By contrast the Roman Catholic Church will only offer Holy Communion to non-Catholics in exceptional circumstances.)
• 'Ecumenical worship', at occasions when Christians of different traditions come together, is no longer often required to be a lowest common denominator, giving offence to no-one, but having little colour or character of its own. Rather, the best traditions of particular churches are used without apology, or, in churches where Christians of more than one denomination regularly worship together, they seek a style which is fresh and creative beyond their inherited traditions.

Today many Christians are discovering and appreciating styles of worship quite new and alien to their own recent traditions. They are often only re-appropriating aspects of their full Christian heritage. The most troubling division remains that between Eastern (Orthodox) and Western (Roman Catholic–Protestant).

BOOKS, ETC.

Avis, Paul (ed.), *The Christian Church: An Introduction to the Major Traditions* (London: SPCK, 2002)

Best, Thomas F. and Heller, Dagmar (eds), *Worship Today: Understanding, Practice, Ecumenical Implications* (Geneva: WCC Publications, 2004)

Butler, David, *Dying To Be One: English Ecumenism: History, Theology and the Future* (London: SCM Press, 1996)

Ellis, Christopher J., *Together on the Way: A Theology of Ecumenism* (London: British Council of Churches, 1990)

Lossky, Nicholas, Bonino, José Miguez, Pobee, John, Stransky, Tom F., Wainwright, Geoffrey, Webb, Pauline (eds), *Dictionary of the Ecumenical Movement*, 2nd edn (Geneva: WCC Publications, 2002)

Wainwright, Geoffrey, *Worship With One Accord: Where Liturgy and Ecumenism Embrace* (New York: OUP, 1997)

Worship and Church Buildings
ROGER BELLAMY

Worship is the fundamental instinct of every person, and closely allied to that is the sense of sacred places and spaces. The Church, for the greater part of its 2,000-year history, has set apart special places for its worship. It needn't have done so. In many climates, those who gather for any activity need some form of shelter, but to create buildings specifically for this activity wasn't essential. But in fact the need for places set apart, for holy places, places where experience showed that God might be encountered, is deeply rooted in the human psyche. The building in most Christian traditions speaks in itself of the faith of its users. Light, space (much more than is required by the liturgy), elaborate design and a feel of permanency have always been features of church buildings. Even the bare and simple chapels of non-conformist Christians have a deep sense of purpose. They express worship focused on the Word of God and congregational hymn singing, just as the medieval church is the place for sacramental worship and the Divine Office, the daily prayers of the church.

Today we ask ourselves what it is we want to express in our worship and what we can create to house that worship. Most parishes find themselves asking how they might re-order their building to make it serve their needs better. In addition to the perceived need of toilets, kitchens, vestries, meeting rooms and so on, the worship space itself may be analysed. The Cathedral in Portsmouth is a good example of how the church building and its arrangements may speak to us. Its theme is a journey and pilgrimage. The nave is an open space, like a market place, where the Christian faith is engaged in dialogue with the world. The figure of Christ hangs over this space. The church isn't a neutral place, but some find faith and through baptism come to be part of the family of God journeying on, empowered by the Holy Spirit. So the nave gives way to a smaller area, under a tower, where the font is located, and that leads us into the main worship space, where there are two focal points: the lectern, for the Word of God and preaching, and the altar, the place of sacrificial offering. Here people stand and sit to be fed by Word and sacrament. Few parishes have the space available in Portsmouth, but that sense of movement, of different focuses, needs to be achieved if at all possible. *Common Worship* services all have an essential shape; gathering, ministry of the Word, response in prayer and the opportunity for sacramental transformation and dismissal. We need to find ways of echoing this shape, and what it can mean for the transformation of our lives in our buildings.

Often our buildings are places of great beauty. They have coloured glass, sculpture, paintings, tapestry, and they speak, not just to our minds, but to our hearts and spirits. Churches also need to challenge us, to ask awkward questions. As Rose Macaulay put it, 'the walls and furnishings tell stories, they instruct and threaten ... they uplift and terrify.' Worship is essential to humanity and requires places of imagination and the numinous, as God seeks to transform his worshippers into the redeemed people he is creating.

BOOKS, ETC.

Bellamy, Roger, *Spirit in Stone* (Durham: Pentland Books, 2001). Copies available by emailing 'stevekingssutton@aol.com'

Giles, Richard, *Re-pitching the Tent* (Norwich: Canterbury Press,1996)

—*Creating Uncommon Worship* (Norwich: Canterbury Press, 2004)

Hammond, Peter, *Liturgy and Architecture* (London: Barrie & Rockliff, 1960)

Macaulay, Rose, *The Towers of Trebizond* (London: Collins, 1956)

WORSHIP AS CELEBRATION

Introduction (15mins)

Welcome and prayer.

Last Session's Challenge

Share your pathway of life and the way being part of the church has shaped it.

Aim of This Session

To explore worship as celebration.

Liturgy

The Gathering: The Easter Acclamation

Alleluia. Christ is risen.
He is risen indeed. Alleluia.

Reflection (20mins)

Share how your church worships.

• What happens, what is included, what it does to and for you, who takes part, etc.?
• What are the similarities and differences between this and other 'great events' such as a cup final match, a royal visit or a pop concert?
• What are the effects of proclaiming this acclamation in your lives as disciples of Christ?
• How could the worship of your church and life speak more of celebration and glory?

Bible Bit (20mins)

Revelation 4
(This passage follows the judgement of the seven churches of Asia Minor and is an invitation to get a heavenly perspective on worship.)

- What is the writer trying to convey about the context, character and effect of Christian worship?
- What connection is there between this vision of worship and your experience of church worship?
- How could the worship of your church reflect more clearly the worship of heaven pictured here?

Share Spot (15mins)

Talk about the Share Spot resources for this session, which explore the world in which we worship and the challenges of being a parish church in this sort of world.

- What can we learn from other faiths about worship?
- How would you describe 'parish worship'?

Ponder Point (5mins)

What has this session clarified about your discipleship?

Prayer (5mins)

Challenge

- Find time this week to record what you have learned from this session.
- Write down three ways your life might better celebrate the glory of God.
- Ask God for help to live this way.
- Prepare for the next meeting by going through the next session.

Share Spot Resources

Worship and Other Faiths
ROBERT BEARD

Worship, defined as 'the offering of devotion, praise and adoration to that which is deemed worthy of such offering, usually God' is naturally familiar to adherents of those faith traditions which are founded on a belief in God, including Judaism, Christianity, Islam and Sikhism, and their various derivative strands and sects.

Worship is perhaps harder to identify in those faith traditions which ascribe either a lesser place or (at least theoretically) no place at all to the concept of a divine being or beings. The compulsion of believers to express their experiences of awe, reverence and gratitude is nonetheless visibly present in most of these too; in particular forms of Buddhism, for example, adherents demonstrate veneration and gratitude towards the Lord Buddha, revering his relics and other symbols of his presence, even though he himself may be understood to be beyond receiving such devotion.

This suggests that an important root of the human compulsion to worship is a sense of dependence upon the object of our worship; dependence for our existence, for those experiences and goods that make our existence worthwhile, and for the fulfilment, either as individuals or as communities, of our ultimate purpose, however that may be conceived.

In most faith traditions, particular forms of language and ritual have evolved to evoke the experience of worship and to express the special nature of what is being offered. The mind and heart of an adherent may be engaged in many ways, through the solemn reading of scriptural texts, through the sight of exquisite ornamentation in the place of worship, through the fragrance of flowers and incense, through the sounds of voices or drums, bells and other musical instruments, through the movements of those leading worship and the worshippers themselves – and perhaps above all through a sense of belonging to a particular identifiable tradition and/or community.

Although the practices associated with worship vary enormously among – and within – the different faith traditions, experience of interfaith dialogue indicates that patience and an open-minded, open-hearted desire to understand others' traditions will often result in a recognition that the desire to worship is common to many cultures, and the exploration of each other's doctrines and practices can be both fascinating and enormously fruitful.

Increasingly, adherents of different faith traditions are expressing the desire to worship together; a desire, which is usually met with caution – and sometimes with suspicion or even hostility – by faith community leaders. Where this desire exists, it should perhaps be expressed gradually. Visits to each other's places of worship, and the sharing of readings from sacred texts may lead on naturally to praying in each other's presence, and so ways of worshipping together may evolve quite naturally among those who have taken time to form relationships of love and trust across traditional faith divisions.

BOOKS, ETC.

Aria, Tosh, and Araijarah, Wesley (eds), *Spirituality in Interfaith Dialogue* (Geneva: WCC Publications, 1989)

Bowker, John (ed.), *The Oxford Dictionary of World Religions* (Oxford: OUP, 1997)

Disbrey, Claire, *Listening to Other Faiths* (Oxford: Bible Reading Fellowship, 2004)

Ipgrave, Michael (ed.), *The Road Ahead: A Christian-Muslim Dialogue* (London: Church House Publishing, 2002)

Race, Alan, *Interfaith Encounter* (London: SCM, 2001)

Smoch, David (ed.), *Interfaith Dialogue and Peacebuilding* (Washington DC: United States Institute of Peace Press, 2002)

Parish and Worship
JOHN THOMSON

The word 'parish' comes from the Greek word *paroikos* meaning 'a temporary resident'. Initially it referred to migrant workers who were transitory people, non-residents of their society. The word we call 'church' or *ekklesia* was originally the citizens' assembly, i.e. the assembly of those who belong. To integrate *ekklesia* or church with *paroikos* was about bringing the migrants into the assembly of those who belong, in this case to God. It was about enabling outsiders to become insiders. Hence in some sense parishes represent a tradition which speaks of a home for the homeless and of being communities of guests, invited by God to enjoy divine hospitality. What, historically, was a word focused around the people has now become associated with place. Both matter, since the incarnation (the Christian conviction that in Jesus God became flesh at a particular time and place) means that locations as well as lives matter to God. Parishes are like the mission stations of the diocese, the Anglican local church. The present structure of parishes traces its roots to the initiatives of the last Greek-speaking Archbishop of Canterbury, Theodore of Tarsus, who, in the seventh century divided what we call England into dioceses and parishes. In some sense, therefore, England is an ecclesiastical concept. Before this, it simply represented a series of conflicting kingdoms.

Parish worship therefore is about enabling people to experience the hospitality of God in a way that builds their lives into his community, the church. The liturgy represents the public expression of this process: a common liturgy, since it is the joint worship of clergy and laity (in reaction to the perceived clericalism of the medieval church), and is also agreed upon by the community as a whole. Over the long history of Christianity in England, parish worship has represented continuity and change. Until the Reformation of the sixteenth century, the discipline of worship followed the traditions of the church centred in Rome. Thereafter a process of exploration led to the distillation of Archbishop Thomas Cranmer's revisions into what we call *The Book of Common Prayer*. This remained the principal expression of public worship in the Church of England until the twentieth century, when a number of revisions including the 1928 Prayer Book, the services which were distilled into *The Alternative Service Book 1980* and, most recently, *Common Worship* arrived. In addition, the legacy of various church traditions is evident in the way worship is enacted, varying from very informal 'low church' expressions to very carefully choreographed 'high church' practices.

Parish worship is therefore more varied now than ever. However, its roots remind us that this is the context where all of us are spiritual vagrants invited to share in God's hospitality. Hence parish worship needs to facilitate this encounter, combining the local and catholic in an accessible yet accountable form. The liturgies provide a skeleton. Parishes have the challenge of expressing the distinctiveness of their worship in creative and accessible ways to those whom God is inviting to join his *ekklesia.*

BOOKS, ETC.

Craig-Wild, Peter, *Tools for Transformation: Making Worship Work* (London: Darton, Longman and Todd, 2002)

Davie, Grace, *Religion in Britain Since 1945* (Oxford: Blackwell, 1994)

Eastman, Michael and Latham, Steve, *Urban Church: A Practitioner's Resource Book* (London: SPCK, 2004)

Jenkins, Timothy, *Religion in English Everyday Life: An Ethnographic Approach* (Oxford: Berghahn Books, 1999)

Thomson, John B., *Church on Edge? Practising Christian Ministry Today* (London: Darton, Longman and Todd, 2004)

Williams, Rowan, *Why Study the Past? The Quest for the Historical Church* (London: Darton, Longman and Todd, 2004)

WORSHIP AS SERVICE

Introduction (20mins)

Welcome and prayer.

Last Session's Challenge
Share the three ways your life might celebrate the glory of God which you recorded over the past week.

Aim of This Session
To explore the link between worship, service and vocation.

Liturgy

The Gathering
Almighty God,
to whom all hearts are open,
all desires known,
and from whom no secrets are hidden:
cleanse the thoughts of our hearts
by the inspiration of your Holy Spirit,
that we may perfectly love you,
and worthily magnify your holy name;
through Christ our Lord.
Amen.

Reflection (20mins)

- What does 'being called to worship' mean to you?
- How does praying this prayer shape your understanding of vocation?
- What do you think this implies for your local church, the church in society, your life?
- Think of other times in your life when you've been called to do something – e.g. jury service, national service, the washing up, etc.

- What was your response to this call?
- What made you respond that way?
- How did you feel afterwards?
- What did that call do to you?
- How does seeing your life as a vocation, a calling from God, help you understand discipleship better?

Bible Bit (20mins)

1 Peter 2:9–10
(In this passage St Peter sets Christians' struggles and suffering in the context of their calling as a distinctive holy people.)

- What does this passage suggest about vocation?
- How does it relate to what you have already shared?
- How does it challenge what you have already shared?
- How has the church lived up to its calling in your area?

Share Spot (15mins)

Talk about the Share Spot resources for this session, which explore some possible out-workings of Christian vocation.

- What does it mean for your discipleship to carry the cross?
- How do or how did you express your discipleship calling at work?
- What distinguishes a calling to public ministry, lay or ordained, from discipleship?

Ponder Point (5mins)

What has this session clarified about your discipleship? Reflecting on the last three sessions, how do you understand discipleship now?

Prayer (5mins)

Challenge

- Find time this week to record what you have learned from this session.
- Look at the gifts you have been given, the gifts present in your church and the challenges you face as a Christian and a Christian community where you are. Write a 'vocation statement' for your life and for your church in terms of these gifts.
- Prepare for the next meeting by going through the next session.

Share Spot Resources

Vocation and Discipleship

JOHN THOMSON

Some time ago I received a copy of *National Geographic Magazine*. It contained fascinating articles on subjects ranging from ancient Egyptian civilisation with pyramids and pharaohs to the Mardi Gras celebrations of New Orleans, taking in along the way stunning photography of grey sharks and an Arctic expedition. In the middle of the section on New Orleans was a paragraph describing a young downtown street evangelist. Carrying an old wooden cross, he exclaimed, 'You've got to be called to do this!'

Christian discipleship is about being called to follow Christ and to carry the cross. Certainly those who sought out the grey sharks or slogged across the Arctic had a sense of vocation. Yet this was a challenge they set themselves. Following Christ and carrying the cross is something the young street evangelist felt came to him from beyond himself. It was his calling from God and he obeyed.

Discipleship is expressed in different ways depending upon the contexts we find ourselves in. Nevertheless, however we live out this calling, it will always be about pointing to Christ. Like John the Baptist, our lives should say 'he must increase, I must decrease' (John 3:30). The Church Army is a good example of practical discipleship being put into action. Their founder, Wilson Carlile, felt compelled to share the faith with those who were outside the nineteenth-century Church of England's congregations. Hence in 1882 he set up the Church Army and later said of its work, 'We do not seek to drag the Church of England into the mud, but to bring some of the social mud into the church.' In sharing the faith, Carlile and his fellow evangelists found that their own discipleship took on a distinctive character. It was not simply about street preaching but also about social provision. It was not simply 'talking the talk' but also 'walking the walk'. To be disciples of Jesus, is, like him, to walk alongside people and love them as God loves them.

Being disciples demands our all. St Paul calls Christians 'slaves of righteousness' (Romans 6:16–18) and the signing of the cross in baptism is the symbolic branding of the disciple with the sign of Christ's ownership. This is why Jesus described discipleship as being called to take up a cross. To do so was to say that your whole life was now given up. Nothing was left to you but this journey. You had died to other ambitions. Thus discipleship is a costly call and one which we can only live out faithfully as part of that great company of disciples we call the church. As Jesus taught us, the first word of the Lord's Prayer is 'Our' rather than 'My' Father in heaven. Thus worship and discipleship go together, since faith is like a pendulum. In worship we swing towards Jesus to be nourished and resourced so that as we swing back to our daily lives, we are able to share his love with those we meet. Indeed, it is as we embody the character and love of God that our words about God have bite. As in the Eucharist, Jesus takes us, like the bread, blesses us, breaks us and shares us.

BOOKS, ETC.

Alison, James, *Knowing Jesus* (London: SPCK, 1998)

Bonhoeffer, Dietrich, *The Cost of Discipleship* (London: SCM, 2000)

Brown, David, *Discipleship and Imagination* (Oxford: OUP, 2004)

Called to New Life: The World of Lay Discipleship Report (London: Church House Publishing, 1999)

Gilbert, Peter, *Walk the Walk: Radical Discipleship through Holiness* (Farnham: Crusade for World Revival, 2004)

Hauerwas, Stanley, and Willimon, William H., *Resident Aliens: Life in the Christian Colony* (Nashville TN: Abingdon Press, 1989)

—*Where Resident Aliens Live: Exercises for Christian Practice* (Nashville, TN: Abingdon Press, 1996)

Jones, Thomas, *Strong in the Grace: Reclaiming the Heart of the Gospel* (Waltham, MA: Discipleship Publications, 2004)

Morley, Patrick M., *Discipleship for the Man in the Mirror* (Grand Rapids, MI, Zondervan, 2002)

Walton, Steve, *A Call to Live: Vocation for Everyone* (London: Triangle, 1994)

Watson, David, *Discipleship* (London: Hodder & Stoughton, 1983)

Vocation and Work
GORDON MORTON

For many Christians, the workplace is where they spend a large part of their time. As disciples, we cannot suddenly divorce ourselves from our faith at nine o' clock on a Monday morning. There are many issues facing the Christian in the workplace.

First, those in employment spend a large part of life with those who are not Christians or at least not churchgoers. Work therefore becomes a context where faith is challenged. Do we conform to society's standards? Or do we witness to the standards and ethics of the Kingdom of God and attempt to transform those fallen structures in which we work?

Perhaps it all boils down to two options: keep quiet about our faith and accept the world's standards or stand up and be counted as a Christian. Both can cause problems for the Christian. The former may cause us to consider imitating the betrayal of Jesus by Peter as he denied three times that he had a relationship with the Master. The latter may set us apart from our colleagues and place us in difficult situations.

If we take the second option, we are living the life of a disciple in the world. As the Old Testament character, Daniel, discovered this world may not be entirely bad but there are times when it is difficult to conform to its norms without compromising our beliefs.

Yet in the workplace there are many opportunities to serve God. There are opportunities to witness to those who do not know Jesus, through sharing testimony or through acts of service. We can develop our own God-given ministries in order to serve our colleagues. This may be being a shoulder to cry on or buying a colleague a cream cake if we know they are feeling low. For those with other gifts there may be the opportunity to serve as Trades Union officials or First Aiders, taking on the jobs people might not usually care for.

For Christians in authority and power there are ethical issues at stake. Using the Kingdom's resources in a way honouring to God may not always be the easiest way to please shareholders. Accountability is a real issue and in extreme cases pressure to increase profits may involve compromising faith. Martyrdom may seem very noble but it rarely pays the mortgage. There may also be occasions when Christians are called to discipline people. Perhaps the company structures are not in line with biblical values. There may be occasions when Christian managers are asked to make their employees redundant. In this situation the support of their faith and their church is crucial.

Sometimes work is glamorous, exciting and fulfilling. At other times, work involves drudgery. Nevertheless, Christians are called to be salt and light in the workplace. Even if society describes a job as lowly or menial, it is still a chance to honour God and on occasion this may even be our vocation. Our own personal gift of holiness can be expressed in our attitudes to the workplace and to our colleagues. It is not a case of passivity. God may call us to challenge those fallen structures within which we struggle.

These are some of the issues and challenges facing Christians in the workplace. The Church is there to nurture growth in discipleship and support those members who spend most of their time in the secular world.

BOOKS, ETC.

Beckett, John, *Loving Monday* (Leicester: Inter-Varsity Press, 2001)
Greene, Mark, *Thank God It's Monday* (London: Scripture Union, 2001)
—*Supporting Christians at Work* (Sheffield: Administry, 2001)
Kellet, David, *Champions for God at Work* (Bradford on Avon: Terra Nova, 2001)
Larive, Armand, *After Sunday, a Theology of Work* (New York: Continuum, 2004)
Oliver, David and Thwaites, James, *Church that Works* (Milton Keynes: Word Publishing, 2001)
Ryken, Leland, *Work and Leisure in Christian Perspective* (Oregon: Wipf and Stock, 2002)
Sprunger, Ben, Suter, Carol and Kroeker, Wally, *Faith Dilemmas for Marketplace Christians* (Scottdale: Pennsylvania, 1997)
Stevens, R. Paul, *The Abolition of the Laity* (Carlisle: Paternoster 1999)
Stokes, Andrew, *Working with God: Faith and Life at Work* (London: Mowbray, 1992)
Thomas, Keith (ed.), *The Oxford Book of Work* (Oxford: OUP, 1999)
Volf, Miroslav, *Work in the Spirit: Towards a Theology of Work* (Oxford: OUP, 1991)

Vocation: Lay Ministry
JOHN BOUCH

In the most significant sense, all Christians from their baptism have a vocation to serve Christ in life. Hence every Christian has a vocation and part of the responsibility of each Christian is to seek out that vocation through worship, prayer, conversation and, ideally, spiritual direction.

There is also an increasing recognition of the important contribution which lay people are making to the ministry of their parishes. In many cases this is the kind of activity which Christian people in all generations have undertaken as a natural result of being who they are and responding to the needs of those around them. It often goes unrecognised by the church, but is valued by those who receive it. Alongside this has developed an increasing awareness among some people that they are being called to do something more formal, which may become part of the 'official' ministry of their church. Knowing that what they do is recognised by their church and by their Bishop helps to make this clear for themselves and for those with whom they work.

For some, who take part in leading the worship of their church or preaching, their ministry will be worked out as Readers. For others, whose sense of calling leads them to respond to the needs of people in the community or the church, it will be undertaken as a Pastoral Worker or Assistant. Others who find themselves able to share their faith with others may become Lay Parish Evangelists. In addition, there are the essential ministries of children's leaders and youth work leaders and, in time, we may hope to see other forms of episcopally authorised lay ministry emerge. It is important to recognise that, although they take different forms, all these kinds of ministry contribute equally to the life of the parish and beyond.

The precise direction which each person's ministry will take needs to be worked out in the parish by taking account of each person's unique gifts, the needs of the communities within the parish, and the parish's own 'mission statement'.

BOOKS, ETC.
Avis, Paul, *A Ministry Shaped by Mission* (London: Continuum, 2005)
Called to New Life: The World of Lay Discipleship (London: Church House Publishing, 1999)
Dewar, Francis, *Called or Collared? An Alternative Approach to Vocation*, 2nd edn (London: SPCK, 2000)
Hiscox, Rhoda, *Celebrating Reader Ministry: 125 Years of Lay Ministry in the Church of England* (London: Mowbray, 1991)
Kuhrt, Gordon and Nappin, Pat (eds), *Bridging the Gap: Reader Ministry Today* (London: Church House Publishing, 2002)
Stevens, R. Paul, *The Abolition of the Laity: Vocation, Work and Ministry in Biblical Perspective* (Carlisle: Paternoster, 1999)

Vocation: Ordination
NICK HOWE

A young woman tentatively tells a friend that she is considering becoming a vicar in the Church of England. 'What a waste!' the friend exclaims. The young woman is disconcerted and rather flattered. She thinks of Albert Schweitzer. She had been evading the possibility of priesthood, but people keep asking her whether she's thought about it, and when at last she looks it in the eye, it seems somehow … right. So she pushes a few doors, testing the idea out on people who know her well. No-one laughs at her. She thinks she detects alarm in the eyes of one local vicar, but another is all enthusiasm.

She begins to discuss it with the Diocesan Director of Ordinands, and a Vocations Adviser: people who will journey with her. They seem to honour what she brings, including the uncertainty. In fact neither she nor they seem entirely clear what it might mean for her to be ordained. It seems that the church is in a state of flux: feeling, thinking and praying into a future that will see familiar ways transformed, new patterns of ministry emerging. Exciting times. She begins to suspect there are clergy everywhere asking themselves: 'What am I for?' and she senses how deep that question goes. Some months on, she is starting to feel a little disorientated.

But she is clearer that the process of becoming a vicar (or chaplain, or sector-minister, or non-stipendiary priest) is actually about choosing and being chosen. She is choosing to pursue ordination. She finds it hard to admit, but she has moments when she actually *wants* to be ordained, sensing that it may be fulfilling for her and of service to others. And ultimately, of course, others will choose. At a national conference advisors equipped with rigorous criteria and more information about her than anyone else has ever assembled will make an assessment. They will be interested in her own sense of calling, but just as interested in her spirituality, personality, relationships, leadership skills, understanding of mission and quality of mind: how well she is suited to the being and doing of priesthood. Having received their wisdom, a bishop will decide whether or not she should be trained for ordained ministry.

She finds all this reassuring, despite the possibility of disappointment. A 'No' may be the most gracious word ever spoken to her: she can see that. Then she would be free to explore her life's calling in other ways. A 'Yes' would bring huge changes, but it will not absolve her of her first vocation: to be human in a Christ-like way – it might even make that more difficult.

There is so much for her to think through. But there is no rush, the process may take many months or more. Time to trawl the bookshelves of specialist shops and friendly clergy, for:

Avis, Paul, *A Ministry Shaped by Mission* (London: Continuum, 2005)

Cocksworth, C. and Brown, R., *Being a Priest Today* (Norwich: Canterbury Press, 2002)

Countryman, L. William, *Living on the Border of the Holy* (Harrisburg PA: Morehouse Publishing Company, 1999)

Croft, Steven, *Ministry in Three Dimensions* (London: Darton Longman and Todd, 1990)

Dewar, Francis, *Called or Collared? An Alternative Approach to Vocation,* 2nd edn (London: SPCK, 2000)

Giles, Richard, *How to be an Anglican* (Norwich: Canterbury Press, 2003)

Greenwood, Robin, *Transforming Priesthood* (London: SPCK, 1994)

Jones, Ian J., *Women and Priesthood in the Church of England Ten Years On* (London: Church House Publishing, 2004)

and maybe to watch a film or two: Tarkvosky's *Stalker*, *Priest*, *Babette's Feast*, or even *Spiderman 2*, to help her consider what it might mean to be ordained.

PENITENCE AND PRAYER

LAMENTING LIFE

Introduction (15mins)

Welcome and prayer.

Last Session's Challenge

Share your vocation statement about your life and your church.

Aim of This Session

To explore life in a broken world.

Liturgy

Prayers of Penitence

Our Lord Jesus Christ said:
The first commandment is this:
'Hear O Israel, the Lord our God is the only Lord.
You shall love the Lord your God with all your heart,
with all your soul, with all your mind,
and with all your strength.'

The second is this: 'Love your neighbour as yourself.'
There is no other commandment greater than these.
On these two commandments hang all the law and the prophets.
Amen. Lord, have mercy.

God so loved the world
that he gave his only Son Jesus Christ
to save us from our sins,
to be our advocate in heaven
and to bring us to eternal life.

Let us confess our sins in penitence and faith,

firmly resolved to keep God's commandments
and to live in love and peace with all.

Almighty God, our heavenly Father,
we have sinned against you
and against our neighbour
in thought and word and deed,
through negligence, through weakness,
through our own deliberate fault.
We are truly sorry
and repent of all our sins.
For the sake of your Son Jesus Christ,
who died for us,
forgive us all that is past
and grant that we may serve you in newness of life
to the glory of your name. Amen.

Reflection (20mins)

Talk to the group about what confession means to you.

- What experiences or events make us lament in life?
- How does confession relate to this lamentation?
- Imagine a time recently when someone offended you. How did you feel about them and about your response?
- If you managed to forgive them, what did that involve for you?

Bible Bit (20mins)

Genesis 3
(If this is too long to read, get someone to tell the story dramatically. The story is often called 'The Fall' since it speaks about Adam and Eve 'falling' from their state of moral innocence.)

- How does this ancient story shed light on the creation we are a part of?
- If we didn't have this story, how might we try to 'explain' evil, the tragedies, pain and suffering in this world?
- Is all pain and suffering due to sin?
- How might this passage shed light on the relationship between confession and a broken world?

Share Spot (15mins)

Talk about the Share Spot resources for this session, which reflect on some of the themes raised.

- What does repentance mean in your life?
- What do you say to people who say, 'I can't believe in an almighty loving God in a world like this'?

Ponder Point (5mins)

What has this session clarified about your discipleship?

Prayer (5mins)

Challenge

- Find time this week to record what you have learned from this session.
- For the next session, make a list of things in your local community which cause people living there to lament about life.
- Against each lament, suggest how a Christian community which confesses its sins and knows forgiveness might make a difference.
- Prepare for the next meeting by going through the next session.

Share Spot Resources

Penitential Practices in the Church of England
ROGER BELLAMY

'Repent and believe the Gospel' is at the heart of the Christian life. We are called to change: to recognise our self-centredness. We need to confess our sin, to acknowledge it, and, by identifying it, to do something about it. Our ability to delude ourselves is extraordinary. Our admission that we are sinners in need of the mercy of God requires a fundamental attitude within us, of penitence and faith. We do not simply admit our sins of omission and commission, but express faith that through the death and resurrection of Christ God has put things right.

In the Church of England we have almost entirely relied on *general confessions* for this purpose. *The Book of Common Prayer* has a penitential feel to it and prayers of confession are important elements of every service. The language is often specific, and to our modern ears, sometimes inappropriate. Getting the balance between being sinners and forgiven sinners is hard. 'The Prayer of Humble Access', for example, speaks of us as 'unworthy' despite our very recent absolution. *The Alternative Service Book 1980* and now *Common Worship: Services and Prayers for the Church of England* continue this reliance on general confession. It is required at principal services, and must be in authorised words. The newer prayers express our penitence in less profound ways, but *Common Worship* does emphasise the need for preparation for worship and focuses that in confession. Pages 161–5 provide 'A Form for Preparation' to be used privately or corporately. These remain general confessions. The great weakness of them is that, even with careful preparation, they become a formula used frequently. We may feel better for having said that we have 'sinned against you and against our neighbour […] we have wounded your love […] We are sorry and ashamed', without having thoughts of any specific occasions of sin. What exactly have we said or done, or thought, through ignorance against our neighbour?

The other tradition in the Western Church is *confession to a priest*. *The Book of Common Prayer* provides this in its service 'The Visitation of the Sick'. The exhortation rubrics make it clear that someone facing death should confess their sins 'if he feels his conscience troubled with any weighty matter'. This tradition has not been much used, but although it was revived with other catholic traditions in the late nineteenth century as a regular practice throughout life, it has again fallen into disuse. *Common Worship*'s material for use with the dying lacks the directness of *The Book of Common Prayer*. A rubric merely says 'the minister may encourage some expression of penitence'.

Confession to a priest is, of course, very much for the living, those who are seeking the mercy of God and growing in their inner lives. It is that self-examination for specific sins of thought and word and deed which is required by confessing to another person. Dietrich Bonhoeffer in *Living Together* quotes St James' admonition to confess to a brother, saying that abandons the 'last stronghold of self-justification and in my brother I meet the whole congregation' (p. 89). Jim Cotter has written *Thanking and Confessing* and provides individual and 'for the whole body' forms. These are very Anglican in spirit. The bringing together of thanksgiving and penitence helps to create a more healthy balance in our lives.

BOOKS, ETC.
Bonhoeffer, Dietrich, *Life Together* (London: SCM, 1954)
Carmichael, Kay, *Sin and Forgiveness: New Responses in a Changing World* (Aldershot: Ashgate, 2003)
The Book of Common Prayer; 'Visitation of the Sick'
Common Worship: 'The Sunday Book and Ministry to the Sick'
Cotter, Jim, *Healing – More or Less* (Sheffield: Cairns Publications 1990)
Dudkey, Martin and Rowell, Geoffrey (eds), *Confession and Absolution* (London: SPCK, 1990)

MacFayden, Alister, Sarot, Marcel and Thiselton, Anthony (eds), *Forgiveness and Truth: Explorations in Contemporary Theology* (Edinburgh: T. & T. Clark, 2001)

Schreiter, Robert, *The Ministry of Reconciliation: Spirituality and Strategies* (New York: Orbis Books, 1999)

Weaver, Andrew and Furlong, Monica (eds), *Reflections on Forgiveness and Spiritual Growth* (Nashville TN: Abingdon Press, 2000)

Theodicy: God and Suffering
DAVID JEANS

Theodicy is the attempt to justify God, particularly in relation to the problem of suffering and evil. The problem: if God is both perfectly good and powerful, why is there evil? Theoretical theodicies try to explain the existence of evil in a universe created by a good and omnipotent (all powerful) God; practical theodicies concentrate on what God does to overcome evil, and what we can do to overcome evil.

THEORETICAL THEODICIES
Many Christians blame suffering and evil on the devil – but, since the devil is created, God must still bear the responsibility. Many more blame it on the Fall and on human sinfulness – but, on any scientific understanding of the history of the world, suffering and death were there long before man appeared on the scene. A more fruitful idea is that evil exists because God gives free will to his creatures. Genuine free will requires that it must be possible for creatures to disobey God.

Linked to this is the idea from science that the universe has freedom to 'make itself', and that many of the 'natural evils' around us (e.g. earthquakes) are a part of the creative process – without earthquakes you cannot have beautiful mountains. This leads to the question of why God allows such freedom. It is argued by many that only with such freedom can human beings make genuine moral choices and grow in goodness. But making suffering and evil part of God's purposes runs the risk of trivialising evil – is not the scale of evil and suffering (Hiroshima, Auschwitz) too vast to allow it as a tool for God's purposes? And why is it distributed so unfairly? Can the joys of heaven justify this much suffering?

PRACTICAL THEODICIES
Practical theodicies often reject the attempt to explain suffering and evil. They point to what God has done and is doing about it, and encourage us to share in overcoming suffering and evil. Wendy Farley believes that we have to recognise the tragedy of suffering. Rather than trying to explain it, we need to concentrate on what God (and we) can do about it. This involves compassion, action and resistance. The cross shows the compassion of God for a suffering world; the resurrection shows that evil can be overcome.

CONCLUSIONS

There are no easy answers to the problem of suffering and evil. The following are the elements of my own wrestling with the issue:

- God permits freedom, suffering and evil because only through the gift of freedom can his final purposes for us and for creation be achieved.
- God suffers with us and weeps with us.
- God has acted and will act to put things right – this creation is not God's final purpose.
- We are called to action in solidarity with those who suffer.

Theodicy is impossible without compassionate action to defeat suffering and evil by God and by his people. Until you have begun to help the sufferer you have no right to 'explain' why he or she may be suffering.

BOOKS, ETC.

(In this area any book that really wrestles with the issues will be difficult, and any simple book will run the risk of encouraging a false glibness.)

Cotterell, Peter, *Is God Helpless?* (London: Triangle, 1996)
Farley, Wendy, *Tragic Vision and Divine Compassion* (Westminster: John Knox Press, 1990)
Hauerwas, Stanley, *Suffering Presence: Theological Reflections on Medicine, the Mentally Handicapped and the Church* (Edinburgh: T. & T. Clark, 1988)
—*Naming the Silences: God, Medicine and the Problem of Suffering*, 2nd edn (Edinburgh: T. & T. Clark, 1993)
Mann, Ivan, *A Double Thirst: Reaching Beyond Suffering* (London: Darton, Longman and Todd, 2001)
McGrath, Alistair, *Why Does God Allow Suffering?* (London: Hodder & Stoughton, 2000)

DEALING WITH DAMAGE

Introduction (15mins)

Welcome and prayer.

Last Session's Challenge

Share with the group your lament list and suggestions from the last session.

Aim of This Session

To explore how confession and absolution enable Christians to live in a damaged world with hope.

Liturgy

Absolution

Almighty God,
who forgives all who truly repent,
have mercy upon *you*,
pardon and deliver *you* from all *your* sins,
confirm and strengthen *you* in all goodness,
and keep *you* in life eternal;
through Jesus Christ our Lord.
Amen.

Gloria

Glory to God in the highest,
and peace to his people on earth.

Lord God, heavenly King, almighty God and Father,
we worship you, we give you thanks,
we praise you for your glory.

Lord Jesus Christ, only Son of the Father,
Lord God, Lamb of God,

you take away the sin of the world:
have mercy on us;
you are seated at the right hand of the Father:
receive our prayer.

For you alone are the Holy One,
you alone are the Lord,
you alone are the most high, Jesus Christ,
with the Holy Spirit,
in the glory of God the Father.
Amen.

Reflection (20mins)

What do the Absolution and Gloria mean to you?

- Imagine you are on a visit to a hospital. Allow your mind to travel around the building. What sorts of people do you see? What sorts of care are being given? What does the place look and feel like? How do you feel about being there?
- Now ask yourself the same questions but instead imagine you are in your church.
- Are there any similarities between a church and a hospital?
- How do the Absolution and Gloria speak of healing in a damaged world riddled with damaged lives?

Bible Bit (20mins)

Luke 8:40–56
(This story is one of a number told by St Luke which involve Jesus dealing with damaged people.)

- Who are the main characters in this story?
- What was their status or position in their society?
- How does Jesus address their damaged worlds?
- Besides their damaged bodies, what else was being exposed for healing in this story?
- How might all this inform your church's ministry of repentance and healing?

Share Spot (15mins)

Talk about the Share Spot resources for this session, which look at ways Christians believe God offers healing for damaged lives.

- What do you believe about healing and its place in the life of your church?

• How should Christians respond to the paranormal?

Ponder Point (5mins)

What has this session clarified about your discipleship?

Prayer (5mins)

Challenge

• Find time this week to record what you have learned from this session.
• Make a list of the ways in which your church is a small sign of God's healing presence in life.
• Prepare for the next meeting by going through the next session.

Share Spot Resources

Church and Healing
GLENN MARTIN

Healing is a word used throughout the Bible and other religious and sacred books. It is a word that has many connotations. Some think of physical cure, some of mental cure, some of spiritual freedom. Healing includes all of these and more. There is the need for salvation, a healing experience in itself. There is the need to address questions of suffering, and of those who with deep faith and goodness still remain in illness and pain. How is it that some suffer and others don't? Is healing the gift of comfort, consolation and strength rather than a cure? Can an inner quality which enables, strengthens and gives inner resolve to combat and endure bring healing to our lives in the absence of a physical cure? What, too, is mental health? How do we decide or describe what it is to be mentally healthy? How does healing fit in here?

Healing needs to be looked at in other contexts, too – employment, housing, environment, diet, relationships, finance. All of these affect us and how we experience life and live it. Do we feel whole and healthy living in squalid conditions? Is the diet we eat helping our bodies to be healthy and function properly? Are relationships causing depression, pain, anxiety, fear, etc.? Where do we need healing here? How we divide our time between work and leisure, or unemployment, can cause stress, ill-health or even death. Balance is needed here, or difficulties of all kinds can arise.

Many talk of salvation as a spiritual healing – a sense of being aware of the presence of God, giving us value, meaning, purpose and the awareness of being loved. This initial experience opens the door for further growth, development and healing in our spirits. Many claim it is about the deepening of their relationship with God, a process of inner healing, involving prayer, sacraments, spiritual direction and retreats.

For some healing is about emotional health, the area of our lives which we feel rather than think. Much of life is lived here and those who are injured emotionally often suffer from depression, lack of energy and apathy or feelings of deep guilt and loss. Despite trying to think positive thoughts and understanding that life isn't 'that bad', they continue to feel low and ill at ease. In the area of sexuality, too, there is often anguish. Marriage and divorce can be a painful area of life, and questions about sexual identity continue to perplex us. How do we define healing here?

What is clear, as we read the Scriptures, is that Jesus was moved with compassion for people. He did heal physically and we know that those who encountered him received emotional, psychological, sexual and spiritual healing. The stories of Jairus' daughter, Lazarus and the Centurion's servant speak of physical healing from illness and death. The stories of the woman at the well (John 4) and the woman caught in adultery (John 8) speak of emotional and psycho-sexual healing. The Church today, in following Christ's commands, needs to find equivalent ways of healing. Stories of prayer, reconciliation, listening and serving in the community (including the health service) are all ways in which we can begin and continue the healing process and fulfil the words of Jesus: 'Greater things shall you do in my name.'

BOOKS, ETC.

A Time to Heal (London: Church House Publishing, 2001)

Burgess, Ruth, and Galloway, Kathy (eds), *Praying for the Dawn* (Glasgow: Wild Goose Publications, 2000)

Cowie, Ian, *Jesus' Healing Works and Ours* (Glasgow: Wild Goose Publications, 2000)

Evans, Abigail Rian, *The Healing Church* (United Church Press, 1999)

Hacker, George, *The Healing Stream: Catholic Insights into the Ministry of Healing* (London: Darton, Longman and Todd, 1998)

Hughes, Gerard W., *God of Compassion* (London: Hodder & Stoughton, 1998)

Parker, Russ, Fraser, Derek and Rivers, David, *In Search of Wholeness* (Nottingham: St John's Extension Studies, 2000)

Tuckwell, Gareth, and Flagg, David, *A Question of Healing: The Reflections of a Doctor and a Priest* (Guildford: Eagle, 2000)

Wilkinson, John, *The Bible and Healing: A Medical and Theological Commentary* (Michigan: Eerdmans, 1998)

Willows, David, and Swinton, John (eds), *Spiritual Dimensions of Pastoral Care* (London: Jessica Kingsley, 2000)

The Church and the Paranormal
CHRISTOPHER SMITH

The Christian Church is uniquely equipped to deal with paranormal phenomena. The victory of Christ over sin, evil and death effected by the sacrifice of Calvary is an ultimate one in all services of the Word. It is the given, both temporarily and eternally; it is the context within which a Christian ministry in this area should be exercised. Normally, this ministry is described as the 'ministry of deliverance', which is by far the best term to use. It is a ministry exercised by the whole people of God. The ordained priest is commissioned by the Church to offer specific liturgical actions (blessing, minor exorcism, prayer, the celebrating of Requiems) which form the reality of the eternal truth of God's power and love for all his creation expressed and wrought upon the cross by Jesus, victor and saviour.

PARANORMAL ACTIVITY
People will tend to present themselves for help with the following types of activity:

* Poltergeists: inexplicable movements of objects, electrical abnormalities within the home and other examples, which can best be described as displaced kinetic energy.
* Place memories or ghosts: strange, normally visible experiences of people which seem to be permanently associated with one particular place.
* Unquiet spirits: the experience of the presence of a particular person who has died, often in unusual or tragic circumstances and who may or may not be known to the individual affected.
* A sense of oppression: feelings of being oppressed by malign forces or individuals, which often have specific physical manifestations.
* Possession: a sense on the part of the presenting individual that in some way or another they have been taken over by or are being controlled by a demonic presence.

SPECIFIC MINISTRY
In nearly all of the above types of experience, the proper person to exercise the ministry of deliverance is the parish priest. It is normally desirable that the priest involves mature and discerning Christian members of the local community in this ministry. Occasionally, it will be necessary to consult the Bishop's adviser, who will endeavour to facilitate the local priest's ministry, and can act as a type of back stop or bench mark in tricky situations. Only rarely is it necessary to involve the adviser in the specific ministry of deliverance. If such involvement is appropriate, the decision will always be taken collaboratively and after considerable mutual consultation.

SIMPLE GUIDELINES

- Always (whatever your particular theological stance) take the presenting person seriously.
- Keep careful notes of any conversations, meetings or visits.
- Never be rushed into action, however demanding the person asking for help may be.
- If necessary (invariably with personal and place-based phenomena) check the basic facts, e.g. the person's medical and personal history.
- Never suggest demonic possession if the person has not articulated it themselves.
- Avoid any suggestion that what is offered in deliverance is a form of Christian magic.

BOOKS, ETC.

A Time to Heal (London: Church House Publishing, 2000)

Deadman, Fletcher, and Henderson, Oliver (eds), *Pastoral Prayers* (London: Mowbray, 1996)

MacNutt, Francis, *Healing* (London: Ave Maria Press, 1991)

Parker, Russ, and Mitton, Michael, *Healing Wounded History* (London: Darton, Longman and Todd, 2001)

Perry, Michael, *Deliverance: Psychic Disturbance and Occult Involvement* (London: SPCK, 1996)

SESSION 3

A PRAYING PEOPLE

Introduction (15mins)

Welcome and prayer.

Last Session's Challenge

Share your thoughts on how your church is a healing sign.

Aim of This Session

To explore the work of prayer.

Liturgy

Prayers of Intercession for the Church of Christ, Creation, human society, the Sovereign and those in authority, the local community, those who suffer, the communion of saints.

The Lord's Prayer

Our Father in heaven,
hallowed be your name,
your kingdom come,
your will be done,
on earth as in heaven.
Give us today our daily bread.
Forgive us our sins
as we forgive those who sin against us.
Lead us not into temptation
but deliver us from evil.
For the kingdom, the power
and the glory are yours,
now and for ever.
Amen.

Reflection (20mins)

- What is your understanding of prayer?
- As a group list the various ways prayer happens in and outside a church service.
- Using the letters ACTS (Adoration, Confession, Thanksgiving, Supplication), list when different sorts of prayer happen.
- Share what sort of praying you find most helpful and what sort is most difficult.
- If anyone in the group has been on a retreat, shared in a quiet day or been to a prayer event (e.g. a Night of Prayer), share with the group what it was like.

Bible Bit (20mins)

Matthew 6:9–13

(In Matthew's Gospel, this section forms part of the Sermon on the Mount and falls within a longer section on prayer and discipleship. Luke's shorter version [Luke 11:2–5] is in response to the disciples asking Jesus to teach them to pray.)

- Talk through the Lord's Prayer line by line, looking at the pattern and content of prayer offered here.
- What does this show us about who we are as we pray?
- What does this show us about what is involved in prayer?
- How does your praying as a church reflect this way of worshipping?
- How does this relate to your earlier thoughts?

Share Spot (15mins)

Talk through the Share Spot resources for this session, which focus upon prayer.

- Which way of praying do you find most helpful and why?
- How do you deal with problems in prayer?

Ponder Point (5mins)

What has this session clarified about your discipleship?

Challenge

- Find time this week to record what you have learned from this session.
- Over the next week borrow a *Book of Common Prayer* or *Common Worship* liturgy and use the Offices, Morning and Evening Prayer, as your basis for praying each day. Ask your priest for the Bible readings for the week. If two sessions are too

much, use the Daily Prayer readings and simply pray one office. *(The word 'office' is from the Latin* officium, *meaning 'a work or task', reminding us that prayer is work: the work of the church as the royal priesthood as well as our work in maintaining our relationship with God.)*

* Record what this feels like to you, and what you notice about what is included in these prayers.
* Bring a photocopy of the Nicene Creed to the next session.

Prayer (5mins)

Share Spot Resources

Ways of Prayer
NICK HELM

Prayer is the fundamental sustenance for faith and faithful living. It is intended to connect us to the source of our life, the living water that Jesus talks about with the woman at the well (John 4). We all pray in very individual ways, and yet there are many common ways of praying. However, most of our diets of prayer are pretty limited, and yet the journey of prayer has a menu that is extensive, inviting and exciting, waiting for us to explore. It is common to view prayer as a human activity, with intercession the most common and important way. The disciples asked Jesus, 'Teach us to pray'. Clearly they saw a way of prayer that was more powerful than their own prayer.

There is plenty to explore, perhaps much that could enrich our prayer life further. Prayer is the activity of the Holy Spirit. The Spirit prays in us, so really all we can do is desire this, seek to let it happen, and see where the journey takes us. Here are some key areas to explore in private prayer, whether you are just starting to pray, or have prayed for years.

PREPARATION
Jesus said 'Go into a private place'.

* Where is your private place? Is there a space you have or can make that is private where you won't be disturbed and can focus on being open and as present to God as possible?
* Are you aware of your inner space, that place within yourself that you are in touch with and seek to hold open to God when you pray?
* What posture helps you to pray? Kneeling, using a prayer stool, sitting in a comfortable chair, flat on your back on the floor? Many experienced pray-ers recommend postures where you have a straight back.

• When is a good time to pray, a time when you have energy to be engaged and attentive, you are not too tired and won't be interrupted?

BRINGING SELF TO PRAYER

Prayer is an expression of a relationship between you and God. You are half of this relationship. Who is the you that is coming to prayer? How are you as you start? Where are you (not so much physically, but in your inner awareness of where life has you at the moment)? What are your needs and desires for this time of prayer? What grace from God are you seeking? These are valuable starting reflections as you approach any time of prayer.

STILLING AND TRUSTING

How deeply we enter into prayer depends on all sorts of factors. Taking time to become more still and to let go of immediate concerns helps greatly. This is a process of becoming more present to the truth of the moment. Relaxation exercises are more profound than simply becoming physically relaxed, but can help us mentally to quieten down and open up spiritually to the Holy Spirit. As such they are a profound act of faith, a trusting of all concerns to God while I am giving my attention to God.

Some common ways of stilling are:

• Music: using pieces of music that are calming, gentle, inspiring. There are plenty of collections around with a relaxation theme, but it is advisable to avoid pieces that have strong connections for you to things that are not peaceful.
• Awareness of breathing: take time to listen to your breathing and let it slow to an easy rhythm.
• Awareness of sounds: sit still and focus your listening on the sounds coming from outside, then from inside, then in you (heartbeat, breathing).

USING SCRIPTURE IN PRAYER

Two key approaches to using Scripture in prayer (with roots in the earliest Christian traditions) are *Lectio Divina* and imaginative contemplation, sometimes known as Ignatian prayer.

Both approaches seek to let Scripture speak to us without us having to work at its meaning or application. The meaning and application emerge as a byproduct of the experience of hearing the message of the Scripture for you.

LECTIO DIVINA

This is sometimes called 'slow reading'. Take a short passage and read it slowly, letting each word or phrase sink in. This is a bit like sucking a toffee (rather than using energy to chew it); it requires little effort, just gentle patience as its flavour emerges and is savoured. Where you notice a word or phrase having some impact, stay with it and savour it; let it be God's word for you and hold it in your heart. Don't feel you have to get to the end of a passage. Doing so can distract you from the gift of God for you that you have already received.

IMAGINATIVE CONTEMPLATION

This can be a very powerful way of letting Scripture speak to us. Take a passage (gospel passages are particularly appropriate) and let yourself enter into the story. Use your capacity to picture or imagine the scene. Initially just let yourself be there. Use your senses to see where you are, listen to the sounds, feel the air, smell the aromas, etc., and then slowly let the events of the story unfold with you being involved, perhaps as one of the characters. Spend time at the end in conversation with Jesus about it all.

REPETITIVE PRAYER

Taking a word, a short phrase or sentence and repeating this again and again is another ancient Christian way of praying that is being used more today. 'Jesus', 'Abba', 'alleluia', 'Maranatha', 'prince of peace', 'Emmanuel', or 'Lord' are common, but you can pick your own, as feels appropriate. The Jesus Prayer, 'Lord Jesus Christ, Son of the Living God, have mercy on me, a sinner' is a longer prayer that uses this approach. Say your phrase quietly to yourself or out loud, in the rhythm of your breathing and stay with this for 5–10 minutes or more. Let yourself get to the point where it is happening in you, rather than you doing it. This may take some time. However the art is, paradoxically, not to try to achieve this, but notice when it happens.

SILENCE

Simply be silent in prayer. Aim to be present to God, without the distraction of words, images, activity, and just be. Whenever you become aware of a thought, a distraction, etc., simply notice and let it go, and seek again to be silent and without thoughts. So we enable the Spirit to be tending to things within us that we are unaware of, and we will know the benefit by its effects (which may be noticed long after the event or slowly over time).

REVIEWING PRAYER

Reviewing the experience of your time of prayer can be fruitful and at least as valuable as the prayer itself. At the end of a time of prayer, take a few minutes with a notebook to record what you did, what you were seeking, and any awareness that emerged through your prayer time. What were the high points, what felt significant, what felt difficult or distracted you, how did you feel afterwards? Notice what emerges from these reflections and see if insights emerge. You may wish to turn these into further prayer, thanking God, or asking for grace, forgiveness, help, etc.

Keeping a journal about your prayer experience can be helpful to see how you have journeyed, to return to experiences, and to notice longer-term graces given through your life.

SHARING EXPERIENCE OF PRAYER

While solitary prayer is a very personal experience, there is something profoundly helpful about sharing your experiences. This needs some care, though, as sharing something so personal needs to be honoured and protected. Having a person or group where you can share your experiences honestly and without pressure can enable further growth in your prayer and faith journey. Soul friends, spiritual friends or companions and spiritual directors are all terms that can describe this sort of relationship. They provide a significant opportunity to reflect on your journey and hold yourself accountable for your faith. You may already have someone you know who is able to give you this sort of space; however, if not, it may be helpful to seek someone out. There are many people around who are willing to offer this. It is worth asking around, though many dioceses have someone who can point you to appropriate people.

CONCLUSION

I hope the above ideas provide useful pointers to ways of exploring prayer further. They may stretch, challenge or disturb, but that is what the faith journey is all about. As we are drawn deeper into God we discover new aspects of God in life and experience, particularly in the places we least expect.

Two final points: firstly, it can be very helpful to work out for yourself a foundation for your spiritual life, commonly called a 'Rule of Life'. This needs to be a realistic, achievable minimum you can maintain, daily, weekly, monthly and annually.

Secondly, having a spiritual companion with whom you look at your spiritual life on a regular basis (every two or three months) is profoundly helpful as you have a place to reflect on your explorations, receive support and suggestions for going on.

Enjoy the explorations, but remember, perhaps the best advice in prayer: 'Pray as you can, not as you can't.'

Problems in Prayer
NICK HELM

What we perceive as problems in prayer are no such thing! These so-called problems are invitations and opportunities. Any concerns we have about our prayer life are a very positive sign. They indicate that we are seeking God at a deep level, and that is the key to prayer. Prayer is not always a struggle, but it is often difficult to acknowledge struggling in prayer. It is abnormal not to have struggles with prayer. As with all relationships, there are aspects that will have their difficulties, whether it is making time and space for the relationship, or dealing with the nature of the relationship and ways of attending to it.

Below are some pointers for reflection that may provide ideas for further exploration. I would recommend, as part of the process of exploring and deepening prayer, finding a spiritual companion or guide who will provide personal attention to you and offer suggestions on how to explore prayer.

PRACTICAL ISSUES: SPACE AND PLACE TO PRAYER
These are worth looking at first.

- Place to pray: having a regular place to pray which is only used for prayer can be helpful for those who struggle to pray. Check what distractions may be around. Is there a way of reducing them?
- Boundaries: how protected is your space at the times you want to pray? What can you do to improve this? Do you need to negotiate with those you live with, or turn the phone off when you set aside time?
- Posture: this can make a big difference. Having an upright back has been found to reduce mental distractions. Sitting in an upright chair, using a prayer stool or kneeling may be worth trying.

PERSONAL ISSUES
Getting down to prayer is a very common difficulty, particularly in a world where being productive is the justification we use for our activity. Deep down, we may doubt that we can justify the time spent in prayer when important things need to be done. Do lovers need to justify the time they spend with each other? The practical points above can help this, but there are other issues that emerge that can make it difficult to get down to prayer.

- Busyness: having a busy life, mind, etc. can make it difficult to devote attention to prayer. This can raise issues of lifestyle, but first perhaps it's worth looking at how to slow down, relax and become more still before trying to pray. To spend a few weeks coming to prayer as a time to relax and be still, and not seeking to do anything more, may well help this.
- Inner distractions: those distracting thoughts about what to cook for dinner, or a job you have forgotten to do, can be very irritating when trying to focus on God. How we handle distractions is far more important than not having them. Be relaxed about distractions. When you notice you have been distracted, be gentle with yourself: 'Hey-ho, I've been distracted again'. Notice, and gently let it go, seeking to focus again on your prayer. Persisting in this approach can reduce distractions. Another help can be to have a pad to jot down things you want to remember. You can jot them down and let them go until you have finished praying.

Some distractions can actually be calls to pray about the distracting thought or its roots.

* Trying too hard: being over-intense in any relationship is counter-productive, and this is true in prayer. Try being more relaxed about it. Often this can feel dangerous and yet be the invitation to grow in faith.
* Failure: there can be very strong senses of failure, perhaps over not being able to pray properly, or well, or like others seem to, or not seeing prayers answered. Whatever the reason, notice if this sense is around. Remember, prayer is about relationship rather than achievement. It is the Holy Spirit who prays in us, and so our role is to seek to let that happen, rather than to 'do it yourself'.

There is a real sense in which prayer is wasting time with God. To do this is to show real faith, that God matters more than 'success' and that God's values are not the world's values. This is the sacrifice of worship: letting go of the values of the world, so that we devote ourselves to the values of God.

THEOLOGICAL ISSUES
There are profound theological issues that can affect our prayer and give us huge problems.

* How we see ourselves: seeing ourselves in relation to prayer is a theological issue. In prayer, our relationship is with God, and how we see ourselves will colour how we think God sees us. This can get in the way, and there are all sorts of experiences and attitudes that can cause this.

    Guilt (appropriate or not) can be a major issue here. It can mean that we feel we can't approach God and so we find ourselves reluctant to get down to it. As Julian of Norwich reminds us, sin cannot hinder God loving us, and he looks upon us with pity not with blame.

    If we have a negative self-image caused by experiences of deep wounding in the past, prayer can be a call to bring this for healing. Sometimes though, this can have a kind of arrogance about it – a sense that we are uniquely unlovable by God, in which we say to God, 'You may be able to love them who have failed you, but you have met your match in me. I am the sinner beyond redemption.' Recognising our inner attitudes can take away their power and reduce our struggles to pray, but bringing them to prayer can be important too.
* Our image of God: our image of God (as already described) makes a big difference to prayer. If deep down we have a fearful image of God, we are going to struggle to approach him in prayer. We can have powerful unhelpful images of God in our subconscious, the product of authority figures in our childhood such as parents and teachers. If these were strongly judgemental and unsympathetic characters, we are likely to subconsciously project them upon God and find prayer unattractive and hard to get down to. It is worth pondering the images of God that are around for

you. What is the sense I have as I seek to approach God? What are the feelings that are around? These may be clues to an underlying unhelpful image.

Spending some time with the images of God that Jesus taught (e.g. the Father who likes to give good things) or the images of Isaiah 43:1–4 or Hosea 11:1–4 can be helpful. You can then seek God's grace in healing your image of him.

CONCLUSION

Struggles with prayer are a normal and important part of the journey of faith. Faith will always take us beyond our securities so that our faith can grow. Thus prayer is going to have its points of discomfort. As has been said, 'If you want to walk on water, you have to get out of the boat'! Hopefully these points will help to reduce any sense of stress that you may have about struggling in prayer, and provide some pointers to how to respond to the struggles. Don't forget the value of having someone to share with about what you find happening (or not happening) in your prayer and spiritual journey.

BOOKS, ETC.

Ashwin, Angela, *Heaven in Ordinary: Contemplative Prayer in Ordinary Life* (London: McCrimmon Publishing, 1985)

—*Patterns Not Padlocks: For Parents and All Busy People* (Guildford: Eagle Publishing, 2000)

Cottrell, Stephen, *Praying Through Life: How to Pray in the Home, at Work and in the Family* (London: Church House Publishing, 1998)

Foster, Richard, *Prayer* (London: Hodder & Stoughton, 1992)

Green, Thomas H., *Opening to God* (Indiana, USA: Ave Maria Press 1977)

—*When the Well Runs Dry*, (Indiana, USA: Ave Maria Press, 1998)

Huggett, Joyce, *Open to God* (Guildford: Eagle Publishing, 1999)

—*Finding Freedom* (London: Hodder & Stoughton, 1994)

Hughes, Gerard W., *God of Surprises* (London: Darton, Longman and Todd, 1996)

—*God in All Things* (London: Hodder & Stoughton, 2003)

Jones, Cheslyn, Wainwright, Geoffrey and Yarnold, Edward (eds), *The Study of Spirituality* (London: SPCK, 1986)

Leech, Kenneth, *Soul Friend*, 2nd edn (London: Sheldon Press, 1977)

Linn, Dennis, Linn, Sheila Fabricant and Linn, Matthew, *Good Goats* (New York: Paulist Press, 1994)

—*Sleeping with Bread* (New York: Paulist Press, 1995)

—*Understanding Difficult Scriptures in a Healing Way* (New York: Paulist Press, 2001)

Louf, André, *Teach Us to Pray* (London: Darton, Longman and Todd, 1974)

Magdalen, Sr Margaret, *The Hidden Face of Jesus* (London: Darton, Longman and Todd, 1993)

Metropolitan Anthony of Sourozh, *School for Prayer* (London: Darton, Longman and Todd, 1999)

—*Living Prayer* (London: Darton, Longman and Todd, 1999)

Ramon, Brother, *The Heart of Prayer: Finding a Time, a Place and a Way to Pray* (London: Zondervan, 1995)

Ramon, Brother, and Barrington-Ward, Simon, *Praying the Jesus Prayer Together* (Oxford: Bible Reading Fellowship, 2001)

Runcorn, David, *Choice, Desire and the Will of God* (London: SPCK, 2003)

Silf, Margaret, *At Sea with God* (London: Darton, Longman and Todd, 2003)

—*Landmarks* (London: Darton, Longman and Todd, 1998)

Williams, Rowan, *The Wound of Knowledge*, 2nd edn (London: Darton, Longman and Todd, 1990)

—*Ponder these Things: Praying with Icons of the Virgin* (Norwich: Canterbury Press, 2003)

—*Silence and Honey Cakes: The Wisdom of the Desert* (Oxford: Lion, 2003)

—*The Dwelling of the Light: Praying with Icons of Christ* (Norwich: Canterbury Press, 2003)

Yancey, Philip, *What's So Amazing About Grace?* (Michigan, USA: Zondervan, 1997)

THE LITURGY OF THE WORD

THE BIBLE AS HEARING AID

Introduction (15mins)

Welcome and prayer.

Last Session's Challenge
Share what praying the Offices has been like.

Aim of This Session
To learn how to listen to Scripture.

Liturgy

Lectionary Readings. *(The lectionary is the calendar of readings which the Church follows over the course of a year. It helps us to follow the story of the Scriptures.)*

Reflection (20mins)

- What does it mean for you to listen to God's word?
- Where and how are the Scriptures listened to in your church?
- How could your church be helped to listen more enrichingly?
- Think about how you learned to speak English or your mother tongue: who helped you and with whom did you learn it?
- Are there any similarities between this and the way we learn to listen to Scripture?

Bible Bit (20mins)

Contents List of the Bible

- Look at the contents list of your Bible, noting how the books are divided up. Does this tell us anything about the sort of material we find in our Bibles?
- In what kinds of ways do you think the stories of the Bible were listened to in the past?
- What are the challenges or difficulties of reading ancient texts from a different part of the world to our own?

• How does this impact upon listening to God's word as disciples and as church?

Share Spot (15mins)

Talk about the Share Spot resources for this session, which offer suggestions on how to listen to Scripture.

• Which bits of the Bible do you find difficult and how have you found this has helped you hear God's word to you?
• In what ways does the Bible still influence England?

Ponder Point (5mins)

What has this session clarified about your discipleship?

Prayer (5mins)

Challenge

• Find time this week to record what you have learned from this session.
• Choose a book from the Bible that you have never or hardly ever read and come prepared to give a two-minute summary of what you have learned from it. (If necessary have a chat with your minister about it in advance.)

Share Spot Resources

Lectionary Reading
JOHN THOMSON

A lectionary is a book containing extracts from Scripture appointed to be read at public worship. The apportioning of certain extracts for certain days began in the fourth century AD and later still collections were made of readings to be used in the Mass, a process which was completed by the tenth century AD.

The Lectionary used by the Church of England today is rooted in this tradition and in the readings ordered by Archbishop Cranmer in *The Book of Common Prayer*. Readings are provided for Holy Communion (the Eucharist or Mass) and for Morning and Evening Prayer. In Cranmer's view the lectionary meant that the Old Testament was read once a year, the New Testament twice a year and the Psalms once a month. Modern revisions demand less but still intend that Scripture be read throughout in a structured way.

Lectionary reading is a particular challenge to clergy who are committed, through ordination, to using the Offices of Morning and Evening Prayer as the structure for their praying. It ensures that the Scriptures are absorbed by those called to teach in public. Lectionary reading is also a discipline which the church as a whole is called to undertake in public worship. Again, this is to ensure that appropriate Scriptures are read at different times according to the calendar. In *Common Worship*, the calendar provides for two types of time, the Seasons (Advent, Christmas, Epiphany, Lent and Easter) and Ordinary Time (between Epiphany and Lent and from the Monday after Pentecost until the Sunday before Advent). The lectionary in Seasonal Time tends to follow the epic story of God's ways with creation, focused around the ministry of Jesus Christ. Ordinary Time, particularly after Pentecost, uses Scripture to reflect upon the calling of the church. As a rule there is more disciplined reading in Seasonal Time, whilst Ordinary Time allows for more flexibility. Some churches use the latter period to do sermon series on particular books or themes.

Lectionary reading is important for a number of reasons. It ensures that the whole body of Scripture is attended to rather than favourite passages. It enables the pattern of God's ways with creation to be recognised, since the Scriptures represent, in themselves, a wide range of styles and forms of material. It shapes the identity of the church, since we share a common story – God's story – and rehearses this narrative in a way that deepens our awareness of who we are in God's sight. It prevents the Scriptures from becoming pretexts for individual or local agendas.

BOOKS, ETC.
Copies of the Lectionaries of *The Book of Common Prayer* and *Common Worship* can be obtained from SPCK and most Christian bookshops. The lectionary year begins with Advent.

The Bible in England
CHRISTINE GORE

THE BACKGROUND TO THE ENGLISH BIBLE
The Latin version of the Bible, known as the Vulgate, came to Britain in the sixth century with early missionaries such as Columba and Augustine, and this was the accepted Bible of the church in England until the fourteenth century. In medieval England Latin was the language of literate people, so access to the Bible was restricted to the scholars and the clergy. For the ordinary people (and some clergy!) the Bible was a closed book, as they could neither read nor understand Latin.

It was *John Wycliffe* (c.1330–84) and his associates, known as the Lollards, who first attempted to put the Bible into the hands of lay people in their own language. Wycliffe's great desire was to restore the authority of the Bible in the life of the church and nation, and to that effect he believed that the people needed to be able to read and understand the Scriptures for themselves. Although the Church condemned the Wycliffe movement, unofficially their Bible became *the* English Bible of the fifteenth and sixteenth centuries.

The Wycliffe Bible was laboriously copied out by hand and it was not until 1526 that the first printed English New Testament was produced. This translation by *William Tyndale* (1494–1536) was printed in Germany and then smuggled into England where it met with an enthusiastic black market. Tyndale revised his New Testament in 1534 and was in the middle of translating the Old Testament when he was arrested for his 'heretical' work and burned in 1536. Tyndale's 1534 edition of the New Testament was to become the basis of all subsequent English translations until the twentieth century.

In 1535 *Miles Coverdale* produced the first complete printed Bible in English and it was subsequently used by John Rogers at Vilvorde in Belgium, along with Tyndale's New Testament and incomplete translation of the Old Testament, to produce 'Matthew's Bible' in 1537. This was the first English Bible to be published with royal approval, granted by Henry VIII. Coverdale was then commissioned to produce a revision of Matthew's Bible and this 'Great Bible' appeared in 1539, with Henry's blessing and command that it should be in every church so that all could read it.

An extensive revision of the Great Bible was produced in 1560 in Geneva. This 'Geneva Bible' was an immediate success, and became the Bible of the Elizabethan church and of Shakespeare. However, James I did not share the general enthusiasm for this translation and a year after his accession he summoned the Hampton Court Conference, where it was agreed to produce a new version, 'to be read in the whole church, and none other'. Around fifty of the best scholars available were brought together and the resulting King James Bible or Authorised Version (1611) became the most widely read book in the English language for more than three hundred years. A revised version of this translation was made in 1885 to bring it more up to date. This was then extensively revised in the light of new discoveries in the field of biblical scholarship and published in 1952 as the Revised Standard Version.

The Revised Standard Version was still essentially in the tradition of Bible translation going back to Tyndale and no genuinely new translations appeared until the New English Bible in 1970. Its publication in contemporary language marked a new era in English Bible translation. This translation was followed by the Good News Bible (1976), which was designed to be suitable for those for whom English is a second language, and the New International Version (1978) which is currently the bestselling version in English. Many other translations exist, some of which are new translations, such as the New Century Version (1991) and the Contemporary English Version (1995). Others are revisions of older translations, for example the New King James Version (1982) or the New Revised Standard Version (1989).

BOOKS, ETC.

France, Richard T., *Translating the Bible* (Nottingham: Grove Booklets, 1997)
How the Bible Came to Us (London: Bible Society, 1999)
Riches, John, *The Bible: A Very Short Introduction* (Oxford: OUP, 2000)

The Divine Drama
CHRISTINE GORE

Location	Act/Scene	Main Player(s)	Theme
Genesis 1 and 2	Creation	God	And it was good!
Genesis 3—11	De-Creation	Adam, Eve and Noah	Fall and flood
Genesis 11—50	Patriarchs	Abraham	Covenant and promise
Exodus, Leviticus, Numbers and Deuteronomy	Exodus	Moses	Escape from Egypt – liberation and law
Joshua	Conquest	Joshua	Home at last! The Promised Land
Judges, Ruth, 1 Samuel	Judges	Samson and Samuel	Fluctuating fortunes
1 and 2 Samuel, 1 and 2 Kings, 1 and 2 Chronicles	Monarchy	David	The golden era and the darkest hour
Major and minor prophets, Esther, some psalms	Exile	The Prophets and Daniel	Judgement and banishment
Ezra, Nehemiah, Wisdom books	Return	Nehemiah and Ezra	The exiles return – a new beginning for the remnant
The Gospels	Fulfilment	Jesus	Incarnation, redemption and resurrection
Acts	Pentecost	Peter	The church is born – the age of the Spirit is here!
Acts, the Epistles	Mission	Paul	The church reaches out and grows
Revelation	Climax	The Lamb and the Bride	The return of Christ and the new heaven and earth. Consummation.

BIBLE READING

Introduction (15mins)

Welcome and prayer.

Last Session's Challenge

Share your two-minute summary with the group.

Aim of This Session

To explore how the Scriptures are studied and some of the challenges involved.

Liturgy

Hear the Gospel of our Lord Jesus Christ according to N.
Glory to you, O Lord.

Reflection (20mins)

• What do you find challenging about reading the Scriptures?

Imagine that reading the Scriptures is like embarking upon the next step of our journey of life.

• What is involved in looking *behind* the Scriptures as we seek to understand them? (Looking *behind* the passage involves becoming aware of the world it belonged to: its historical context.)
• How do we look *at* the Scriptures as we seek to understand them? (Looking *at* the passage involves becoming aware of its form, type, shape and structure: its literary sense.)
• How do we look *in front of* the Scriptures, at the world they open up, as we seek to understand them? (Looking *in front of* the passage as it sheds light upon the way we are to live life: its contemporary life challenge.)

Bible Bit (20mins)

Luke 4:16–30

Look *behind* the passage:

- What light can you shed on the background to this incident (e.g. the society of the day, the synagogue and Jewish culture and faith, Nazareth and its place in Jesus' ministry and identity, etc.)? It may be helpful for the facilitator to discuss this passage with the minister before the session.
- Where does this passage come from in the Old Testament? How might its historical and literary context have influenced the way Jesus interpreted its meaning?

Look *at* the passage:

- What sorts of writing can you find in this passage and how does this enrich our understanding of it (e.g. prose, poetry, conversation, history, etc.)?
- What sort of situation is described here, e.g. is it one of identity, conflict, surprise, etc.?
- What is this passage's relationship with what has gone before (i.e. the temptations, healings, etc.) and how does this dispose us to interpret it?

Look *in front of* the passage:

- How does this passage challenge you to live as disciples of Jesus today, now that you have some awareness of its historical context and literary character?
- How does this way of reading Scripture enrich your Bible reading?

Share Spot (15mins)

Talk about the Share Spot resources for this session, which look at Scripture reading.

- Which way of reading the Bible do you find most fruitful?
- What is distinctive about reading the Bible as an Anglican?

Ponder Point (5mins)

What has this session clarified about your discipleship?

Prayer (5mins)

Challenge

- Find time this week to record what you have learned from this session.
- Take the three accounts of the story of the temptations (Matthew 4:1–11; Mark 1:12–13; Luke 4:1–13) and devise a Bible study using this schema for a group of teenagers in a club or school.

• As a group arrange to have copies of the Nicene Creed for the next session. This can be found in *Common Worship: Services and Prayers for the Church of England* in the section on Holy Communion, pages 173 or 213.

Share Spot Resources
Ways of Reading and Studying the Bible
IAN DUFFIELD

There are many ways of reading the Bible. Studying the Bible is something that all Christians can do. It is not restricted to so-called educated or intellectual people.

FOCUSING ON KEY TEXTS

The Bible is a long book. Even the new Lectionary has to pick and choose. And we all do, even those who tell you that they don't. Through Christian usage, particular passages appear to stand out for their religious, moral, and practical worth, for example, Exodus 20; Leviticus 25; Psalm 23; 1 Kings 19; Isaiah 6; Micah 6:7; Matthew 5—7; Mark 10:42–45; Luke 10; John 3:16; Acts 4:32–37; Acts 10; 1 Corinthians 13; Galatians 3:28; Colossians 1:20; 1 Peter 3:9: 1 John 4:16; Revelation 21. Read through these passages – are there any others you would like to add?

Not all passages are of equal worth. We may find some passages difficult because of their brutal honesty (uncensored tales of violence and killing without condemnation, taken-for-granted tales of the exploitation of women), or because they seem incomprehensible. Such unproductive passages can be left alone initially, but no one should limit themselves to a few pet ones. Discover those passages that speak, challenge, encourage, uplift, inspire, provoke, call, prod ... those that repay close attention, those with depth, those that you can return to again and again and again. But it will be the witness of the prophets and above all, the ministry, life, death and resurrection of Jesus Christ that will need to be returned to most.

Learn by heart or write down certain passages. Meditate, contemplate, explore: what is this passage saying? On the basis of this passage, what should I be thinking, praying, doing? What is God saying to me through this text? What connection might there be between this biblical passage and my life and the life of my community? Such explorations are assisted by looking up words in a biblical dictionary, reading commentaries on biblical texts, checking out different translations, and by investigating their significance with fellow Christians. On our own we can miss the point, go down a blind alley, chase a red herring, or even totally misunderstand what the Bible says. Others help us to see if we are misguided. Reading and studying the Bible with others is important and helpful.

TRANSLATIONS

The Old Testament was written in Hebrew and the New Testament in Greek. Therefore, a good modern translation is needed to be able to use or study the Bible. College students and official publications tend to use the New Revised Standard Version (NRSV), Evangelicals the New International Version (NIV), and Anglo-Catholics the New Jerusalem Bible (NJB). All of these are helpful. Those who find reading difficult should use the Good News Bible. Other versions can be useful in stimulating reading: J. B. Phillips's translation; Alan T. Dale's *Winding Quest* and *New World*; Hugh Schonfield's *The Original New Testament* and Eugene H. Peterson's *The Message*.

It is helpful to use more than one translation so that they can be compared. This can be important because certain words have a variety of meanings and some passages are difficult to convey in English. All translations involve some level of interpretation, and some translations have been unintentionally sexist in referring to human beings as 'men' (note: the NRSV uses inclusive language). So check out how different translations cope with a passage – a lot can be learnt from doing this.

READING OUT, NOT READING IN

There is no neutral or totally objective reading of a passage. We come with pre-suppositions and assumptions, with needs and concerns. These will affect the way we read and what we understand a text to be saying. Although there is never only one meaning of a passage, the danger is that we will read into a passage what is not there. At its worst, we will make a text say what we want it to say. However, reading the Bible with integrity means seeking to read closely and to read out from a text what is there. A number of factors are involved in this.

Making Connections

The Bible, in many ways, is a foreign document. It comes from different times and places which are in contrast to our own. We, being the people we are, come to a text which is other than us. A conversation can then begin in which we are both true to ourselves and true to the Bible. From this conversation we may find that there are *connections*, that in some ways (but not others) we can relate to what a passage is saying; and this may have real impact upon us – what we think and what we do.

Understanding the Kinds of Biblical Writing

Being true to the Bible involves understanding a number of things: the kind of writing used (the *genre*), the intention or purpose of the passage and its original social, political, and historical setting. Music takes many shapes and forms from classical music to reggae. The same is true of biblical literature. The Bible is made up of a variety of writing of different kinds: factual, poetic, symbolic, historical, visionary, etc.

It is very helpful to understand what kind of writing you are reading or studying. Poetry is obviously different from history. Furthermore, we should not expect to find either science or history in any modern sense in the Bible, because these have only emerged in the last three hundred years. So Genesis 1 and 2 are not natural science or biology; and 1 and 2 Kings are not straight reportage of history (for example, hardly anything is said about Omri, a major king – this is like describing the royal family in England in the twentieth century with only a cursory mention of Elizabeth II). Often, there is a mixture of historical recollection, theological perception and spiritual insight. The history of nations as well as the community of faith is interpreted in the light of God's liberating purposes.

Much of the prophetic literature is assertion of religious, communal, and political consequences rather than reporting of future history, sermons to particular rulers, kings and priests rather than words directly meant for us. Daniel and the Book of Revelation are visionary (or 'fantastic') rather than mundane, coded messages rather than straightforward writing (so Daniel speaks of the Babylonians but is actually talking about the Greeks, and Revelation's fantastic language about beasts, etc., relates to the Roman Empire).

Most of the Epistles are occasional letters rather than theological treatises, spiritual and practical exhortations to particular congregations rather than general instructions for all time. The Gospels are inspiring stories of Jesus of Nazareth rather than biography, and messages of good news rather than works of complicated theology.

In short, the sort of history that appears throughout the Bible is about the community of faith. The stories that are told in the Bible are there to elicit faith, to encourage endurance, to provide guidance for living, to support marginal communities in transition or under pressure and persecution. And they can do that for us too.

Obviously, if someone misunderstands the nature of the text that they are reading they are likely to misread it. Nevertheless, there is no one right interpretation. The Bible is not a compendium of doctrine or ethics, although it provides vital material for each. The Bible is not written about abstract or philosophical matters but about the struggles and experiences of the community of faith in particular historical circumstances.

Reading the Bible from Where We Are
Being true to ourselves also involves certain things. It means reading the Bible in the light of our experience, personal and social, economic and political. Who we are makes a difference to our reading. Women will read the Bible differently from men, working class from middle class, black from white, Third World from First World, poor from rich. All these different ways of reading are important. For too long, the interpretation of Scripture has been in the hands of white, educated men. That is not the only way to read the Scriptures. We need to hear the voices of our brothers and

sisters from different contexts, especially those who are on the margins of life – after all, the early Christian communities were made up of not very important people (1 Corinthians 1:26–29). It can be useful to imagine ourselves reading a text from the perspective of, for example, a poor woman in the Third World, and then return to our own perspective with our horizon of what the passage may be about enlarged.

What does a particular biblical passage look like from my perspective within the community of faith of which I am part: the problems we have to live with, the structures which control our lives, the dreams we have of new life? If we allow the passage to be itself and allow ourselves to be true to where we are, then the dialogue or conversation between us may be very creative.

NEW ATTITUDES AND NEW PRACTICE

The reading and studying of the Bible, at its best, will lead to new attitudes and perspectives, new hope and encouragement, new action and practices, new lives and new community. The Spirit of God inspired the writing of the Scriptures and through the inspiration of the Spirit within us and our communities, the Scriptures can speak afresh in every place, and God's ways with God's people (to which the Bible bears witness) will grow and develop.

BOOKS, ETC.

Davies, John D., *Mark at Work* (Oxford: Bible Reading Fellowship, 1986)
—*God at Work* (Norwich: Canterbury Press, 2001)
Duffield, Ian K., and Pagan, Robin, *Jesus' Radical Torah*, vol. 1 (Sheffield: Urban Theology Unit, 2004)
—*God's Radical Prophet*, vol. 2 (Sheffield: Urban Theology Unit, 2005)
Dunn, James and Rogerson, John (eds), *Eerdmans Commentary on the Bible* (Grand Rapids, MI: Eerdmans, 2003)
Patte, Daniel (ed.), *Global Bible Commentary* (Nashville, TN: Abingdon Press, 2004)
Price, Peter, *Seeds of the Word: Biblical Reflection for Small Church Communities* (London: Darton, Longman and Todd, 1996)
Riches, John, *The Bible: A Very Short Introduction* (Oxford: OUP, 2000)
Wink, Walter, *Transforming Bible Study*, 2nd edn (London: Mowbray, 1990)
The Oxford Bible Commentary (Oxford: OUP, 2001)
Tom Wright's series of commentaries published under the banner of *The New Testament for Everyone* (London: SPCK)
Bible Reading Fellowship materials are very useful (although Evangelicals will tend to prefer Scripture Union).

Scripture and Anglicanism
JOHN THOMSON

Scripture has always been prized by Anglicans. The Reformers of the sixteenth century were part of the legacy of the Renaissance's agenda to recover the original purity of ancient traditions, both Greco-Roman and biblical. This manifested itself in a commitment to translating the Scriptures into the mother tongues of the people using the best available resources possible. Where the Bible had been the possession of the educated clergy, the intention now was to make the Scriptures available to the laity. However, the place of Scripture in the discernment of Christian living varied. In terms of the sixteenth-century English Settlement, which came into shape under Elizabeth I and was expressed by Richard Hooker in his *Laws of Ecclesiastical Polity*, Scripture was seen as part of a three-fold conversation through which God's will was made known. This conversation included Scripture, Tradition and Reason. Scripture was understood to be those canonical texts we call the Old and New Testaments, with the Apocrypha regarded as edifying, though not having the same authority as the Testaments. Tradition was regarded as the practices of the Church, particularly as established by the undivided conciliar church. Reason was understood to be 'sound learning'.

Unlike some of the more radical Protestant churches, the Church of England did not regard *sola Scriptura* to mean 'Scripture and nothing else'. Rather, Scripture's task was to act as the light pointing out the way of salvation. However, this 'way' was exhibited and tested by practice and critical thought, just as these were called to account by the light of salvation witnessed to by the Scriptures. Hence Bishops were retained by the Church of England and the relationship between Christian discipleship and society was much more osmotic than in certain of the reformed churches. Furthermore, it was in worship that Scripture was properly grasped and so the lectionary reading of Scripture, the use of Scriptural Canticles and the recitation of the Psalms became central to Anglican practice.

The commitment of contemporary Anglicans to Scripture is evident in the sheer quantity of Scripture in the services of the church. However, discernment of God's call and activity in life emerges through a conversation between the light discerned through close attention to the Scriptures, the way Christian discipleship has been practised over the centuries and what human wisdom is exposing about the character of creation. Anglicans do not hold to an idealistic scriptural blueprint for discipleship, which can be worked out in the abstract for all time. Rather, discernment is dynamic. It is about following the living God, whose presence, in Christ, is witnessed to in Scripture but who is also beyond the confines of Scripture as the active agent of all life. The creation is graced and marked by the presence of God, even in tragedy. Scripture therefore displays the character and story of this God which, though giving us a true vision of God, does not exhaust what God is about. There is a sense that discipleship is a conversation whose focus is in public worship, where all reality is offered to God and where everything is exposed to the bright mystery of Christ, and whose activity is in the bread and butter of daily life.

It is no accident, therefore, that the Church of England as catholic and reformed sought to discover its identity through worship rather than in arguments about precisely how Scripture, Tradition and Reason should be weighted and related. There is thus a provisionality about Anglican theology, not in the sense that anarchy reigns, but in that interpreting is an ongoing, time-consuming experience stabilised but not controlled by the past. Scripture is the first term of this interpretative triad, but is not isolated from the other parts, and all are properly positioned in the environment of worship. It is therefore as Christians gather together in worship that the revelation of God's grace for salvation is known and the capacity to discern the light for the pathway ahead created. This is where Scripture most properly belongs in Anglicanism and where it will do its work, particularly as Anglicanism is now far wider in extent and cultural variety than its English pedigree.

BOOKS, ETC.

Avis, Paul, *The Anglican Understanding of the Church: An Introduction* (London: SPCK, 2000)

Cohn-Sherbok, Dan (ed.), *Using the Bible Today: Contemporary Interpretations of Scripture* (London: Bellew Publishing, 1991)

Dormor, Duncan, McDonald, Jack and Caddick, Jeremy (eds), *Anglicanism: The Answer to Modernity* (London: Continuum, 2003)

Edwards, David L., with Stott, John, *Essentials: A Liberal-Evangelical Dialogue* (London: Hodder & Stoughton, 1988), chapter 2.

Fuller, Reginald H., 'Scripture' in Sykes, Stephen and Booty, John (eds), *The Study of Anglicanism* (London: SPCK, 1988)

Percy, Martyn, *Introducing Richard Hooker and the Laws of Ecclesiastical Polity* (London: Darton, Longman and Todd, 1999)

Radner, Ephraim, *Hope Among the Fragments: The Broken Church and Its Engagement of Scripture* (Grand Rapids, Michigan: Brazos Press, 2004)

Williams, Rowan, *Anglican Identities* (London: Darton, Longman and Todd, 2004)

SHARING THE WORD OF THE LORD

Introduction (15mins)

Welcome and prayer.

Last Session's Challenge
Share your 'Temptations Youth Bible Study' in groups of three.

Aim of This Session
To reflect upon how we share the Word of the Lord.

Liturgy

The Sermon and the Nicene Creed.

Reflection (20mins)

- What do you think is the purpose of the Sermon and the Creed?
- What style of learning best suits you? How might this way of learning be encouraged in your church?
- As a group, using a large piece of paper, list the different ways you share the Word of the Lord at your church. How could this be developed to help others hear the Word of the Lord?

Bible Bit (20mins)

(Ezekiel was an unusual prophet living at the time of the Babylonian exile of Judah in the late seventh and early sixth centuries BC.)
- Divide the group into twos (or threes) and each pair takes one of the following passages: Ezekiel 1; 4; 5; 12. How does Ezekiel share the Word of the Lord in his day?
- Which ways do you find persuasive and why?
- How does this connect with what you wrote on your large piece of paper?
- How flexible should communication's media be for Christians?

Share Spot (15mins)

Talk about the Share Spot resources for this session, which look at imaginative preaching and the way worship and doctrine (teaching) connect.

* What sort of preaching most helps you understand your faith and why?
* What aspects of Christian teaching most appeal to you and which do you find most challenging?

Ponder Point (5mins)

What has this session clarified about your discipleship?

Prayer (5mins)

Challenge

* Find time this week to record what you have learned from this session.
* Take a well-known story from the Bible and imagine a new or engaging way of sharing it outdoors, perhaps in a local shopping arcade or in a street procession.

Share Spot Resources

Imaginative Preaching
JOHN THOMSON

Preaching is:

* a three-way conversation between God, preacher and congregation.
* a worship event – a glorifying of God and his ways with the world.
* an embodied event – drama and theatre rather than simply words.
* a church event – a sharing for now of the wisdom of God for his people.
* an evangelistic event – a sharing with others of the Gospel.
* a contextual event – woven into the details and particulars of life.

Some preaching styles:

* a three-point sermon: usually expository, i.e. exposing the text/theme; a good model, especially for beginners is POINT: PICTURE: PUNCH (point, illustration, application).
* a story sermon: using a story to convey a message.
* a visual sermon: using an overhead or video projector, wallpaper, visual aids, etc.

The key is to let the visual aid support rather than distract from the message.
- a dramatic sermon: using drama either to illustrate or convey a message. Sometimes an interview format can also be used.
- a homily: a short meditation upon a passage or theme.
- a silence sermon: using short verses or phrases to evoke reflection in silence by the congregation.

WARNING!
In all cases make sure visibility and audibility are your friends!
And keep it simple!

LITURGICAL PREACHING

Anglicans are lectionary Christians, i.e. we follow a cycle of readings, which pattern the Christian year. This is important, since calendars not only reflect but form identity. In addition, liturgical preaching faces us with the difficult as well as attractive texts and themes of Christian believing.

BOOKS, ETC.

Coupland, Simon, *Stripping Preaching to its Bare Essentials* (Oxford: Monarch, 2005)

The College of Preachers, 14a North Street, Bourne, Lincolnshire PE10 9AB; website: www.collegeofpreachers.org.uk.

Worship and Doctrine
DAVID JEANS

For many Christians, these two activities have very little to do with each other. Doctrine is often seen as dull, difficult, dry and quite possibly dangerous, whereas worship (we hope) is where we experience the wonder of our faith. In fact the two are closely linked, and need each other. David Watson once said the following of the balance between the place of Word and Spirit in our Christian lives:

All Word and no Spirit – we dry up.
All Spirit and no Word – we blow up.
Both Spirit and Word – we grow up.

The same holds for worship and doctrine.

Doctrine can be dull, difficult and dry if not approached with a sense of worship and wonder. Yet theology involves thinking about God, and surely that should feed and inform our worship. One of the things that can make our faith become stale and dry is if we think that we have God taped, God in a box. St Augustine said: 'If you can understand it, it's not God.'

We need to remember that when we are tempted to give glib and shallow answers about God. God is bigger than us, and all eternity will not exhaust our exploration of him. For me, seeking the answers to difficult questions about God is a place of challenge and growth in wonder at the God whom we worship and serve. Worship can become shallow and even dangerous if not properly informed by doctrine.

How can we avoid our worship being shallow? Worship begins with God and ends with God. In our worship God reminds us of what he has done for us, and we respond to him. When we come to worship we need reminding of God and his love for us. Worship should not begin with how I am feeling, but with who God is and what he has done. We need opening hymns that speak of God and not of ourselves – we need to sing 'You laid aside your majesty, gave up everything for me' before we can respond 'I really want to worship you, my Lord'.

And can worship be dangerous? Arius, the fourth-century church leader who denied that Jesus was properly divine, is said to have spread his heresies through 'catchy rhymes which were sung on the streets'. Many Christians learn their doctrine through their worship, especially today through the songs that we sing. Worship leaders need to think about the words of new songs, and not just about the music!

Doctrine and worship together lead to spiritual growth that keeps head and heart in harmony. In John's Gospel (17:3, NIV) we read: 'This is eternal life: that they may know you, the only true God, and Jesus Christ, whom you have sent.' Worship and doctrine are both ways through which we can grow in our knowledge of God, which will be our eternal task and joy!

BOOKS, ETC.

Cottrell, Stephen and Croft, Steven, *Travelling Well: A Companion Guide to the Christian Faith* (London: Church House Publishing, 2000)

Green, Laurie, *Let's Do Theology* (London: Continuum, 2004)

Gunton, Colin (ed.), *The Cambridge Companion to Christian Doctrine* (Cambridge: CUP, 1997)

Hill, Jonathan, *A History of Christian Thought* (Oxford: Lion, 2003)

McGrath, Alister E., *Understanding the Trinity* (Eastbourne: Kingsway, 1987)

—*Christian Theology: An Introduction* (Oxford: Blackwell, 1995), chapter 14

McGrath, Alister E. (ed.), *The Christian Theology Reader* (Oxford: Blackwell, 1995), chapter 8

Richardson, Alan (ed.), *A Dictionary of Christian Theology* (London: SCM, 1982)

Taizé Community, *Seek and You will Find: Questions on the Christian Faith and the Bible* (London: Continuum, 2005)

Ward, Keith, *What the Bible Really Teaches: A Challenge for Fundamentalists* (London: SPCK, 2004)

Ward, Pete, *Selling Worship: How What We Sing Has Changed the Church* (Milton Keynes: Paternoster, 2005)

White, James, *Introduction to Christian Worship* (Nashville TN: Abingdon Press, 1980)

THE LITURGY OF THE SACRAMENTS: BAPTISM

GAINING ACCESS

Introduction (15mins)

Welcome and prayer.

Last Session's Challenge
Share your outdoor presentation from the last session.

Aim of This Session
To explore the drama of baptism and confirmation. *(If possible this session is best done in a church building. It might be helpful to ask a priest to be present. If you cannot use a font, use a bowl of water where you are meeting, with oils and salt if appropriate.)*

Liturgy

(You will need to have a copy of the baptism liturgy available.)

Reflection (20mins)

Imagine yourselves at a baptism/confirmation service. Using the baptismal liturgy do a baptism/confirmation role play with various members of the group taking the parts.

- What does baptism mean to you?
- What does the symbolism convey to you?
- What do you think happens at baptism?
- How do you think confirmation is connected to baptism?

Bible Bit (20mins)

Matthew 3:13–17, Mark 1:9–11 and Luke 3:21–22
(Each of these passages is situated at the beginning of the ministry of Jesus,

indicating that his baptism and his mission are intimately linked. The temptation stories which follow also display this.)
Using the approach we identified in Section C, Session 2, compare and contrast these three accounts of Jesus' baptism and see how they give insight into Christian baptism.

* Look *behind* the text at the historical context:
  * What sorts of baptisms were around in Jesus' day? (refer to the Share Spot resources).
  * How might John's baptisms have been seen by the rulers of his society?
* Look *at* the text, at its literary form:
  * What can you learn about their respective understandings of Jesus' baptism?
  * What happens to Jesus in his baptism?
* Look *in front of* the text at Christian practice and what it suggests for us today about baptism:
  * How does your understanding of these passages inform your earlier understanding of baptism?
  * What sort of community does baptism make Christians into?

Share Spot (15mins)

Talk about the Share Spot resources for this session, which look at baptismal practice down the centuries.

* What new insights about baptism have you gained from the Share Spot resources?
* Which aspect of the baptism ritual do you find most meaningful and why?

Ponder Point (5mins)

What has this session clarified about your discipleship?

Prayer (5mins)

Challenge

* Find time this week to record what you have learned from this session.
* Look at the 'Renewal of Baptismal Vows' in *Common Worship* pp. 149–51. Imagine explaining to a friend who is not a churchgoer/Christian what each of the vows means for your life and imagine what his or her response might be. Write down your conversation and bring it with you to the next session.

Share Spot Resources

Baptism

EMMA INESON

The 'Pastoral Introduction' to the service of Holy Baptism in *Common Worship* says: 'Baptism marks the beginning of a journey with God which continues for the rest of our lives, the first step in response to God's love'. Baptism is one of the most significant events in the life of a Christian, yet throughout history there have been a variety of understandings of baptism; about what it means to be baptised, how it should happen, and who should be involved.

1. HISTORY AND PRACTICE

Jesus was baptised by John the Baptist in the River Jordan and from then on, baptism has been a central rite of the Christian faith. It was the way in which the first Christians made new disciples. In the earliest church, baptism immediately followed conversion and was the way of signalling belonging to the Christian Church.

During the first century AD, baptism lost some of its immediacy, and some prior preparation began to creep into the rite. Baptisms often took place on Easter Sunday after a long period of preparation during Lent, which involved a great deal of exorcism and dramatic 'scrutinies' (including stripping and standing on goatskin before the clergy who determined whether the candidate was infested with demons!). Baptisms took place at dawn outside the congregation and candidates were brought to the Bishop afterwards. He laid hands on them and anointed them with oil as a sign of the gift of the Holy Spirit.

After Augustine (AD 354–430), who strongly advocated baptising children, there was a rise in the practice of infant baptism. There was a high rate of infant mortality and Augustine was concerned that no child should die unbaptised and therefore 'unsaved', as he saw it. Many of these baptisms were carried out at the time of birth by midwives. It was difficult for Bishops to get round all the parishes to perform the laying on of hands and anointing, and so a time lag between baptism and 'confirmation' of that baptism by the Bishop (and therefore the taking of Holy Communion) arose.

The Reformers continued to baptise infants, and the backdrop of religious division (Romans Catholics on the one hand and nonconformists on the other) added urgency to the perceived need to baptise as many people as possible according to the rites of the Church of England. The baptismal rites of the 1662 *Book of Common Prayer* remained the only legal ones until 1966, when alternative services began to be introduced.

As society and culture change, so does baptism practice. Today, it is no longer the case that all, or even most, people will undergo Christian baptism. Secularisation and a multi-faith society have led to a decrease in the number of infants being baptised. However, there has been an increase in the number of adult candidates for baptism and confirmation. Baptism preparation and practice has changed to accommodate this fact. In *Common Worship*, provision is made for a variety of initiation services, reflecting the current diverse context. A Service of Thanksgiving for the Gift of a Child, Holy Baptism for adults and/or children and Services of Baptism with Confirmation are all provided to meet a variety of liturgical and pastoral situations.

How the water is actually administered has changed over time. In the very beginning, people would have been baptised in running water (such as a river). With the institutionalisation of Christianity, still water in containers (baptistries and fonts) was increasingly used. The common practice in the earliest church was to immerse candidates fully in water – even babies (unless they were very frail). The Reformers saw full immersion as the first option, with 'pouring' as a fallback for the weak. But from then on fonts became increasingly smaller and sprinkling became the norm. With the rise in the number of adult candidates, there has been an increased interest in baptism by full immersion. Various means have been found for doing this in churches without baptistries (including hiring birthing pools!).

2. THEOLOGY AND LITURGY

The theology and symbolism of baptism are rich and varied and the liturgy for baptism reflects this fact. Here are some key themes (all the liturgy extracts are from *Common Worship* and Bible references are from the *New Revised Standard Version*):

The Body of Christ

For in the one Spirit we were all baptised into one body …

(1 Corinthians 12:13)

Faith is the gift of God to his people. In baptism the Lord is adding to our number those whom he is calling. (From 'The Presentation of the Candidates')

Baptism is the way in which the candidate becomes a member of the Church, the body of Christ. It therefore involves everyone present at the service, as well as the wider Church. Thus the whole congregation pledges its support at the Presentation of the Candidates: it shares with them in professing their faith, and it welcomes the newly baptised into the 'fellowship of faith'. This is the reason that many fonts are situated near the doors of a church – their point of entry.

New Birth

Blessed be the God and Father of our Lord Jesus Christ! By his great mercy he has given us new birth into a living hope through the resurrection of Jesus Christ from the dead. (1 Peter 1:3)

Our Lord Jesus Christ has told us that to enter the kingdom of heaven we must be born again of water and the Spirit, and he has given us baptism as the sign and seal of this new birth. (From 'The Introduction')

At baptism, there is a sense in which we begin our Christian life; our life in God. It signifies the 'new' birth Jesus told Nicodemus about (John 3:3). As with any 'life beginning', the next steps are growth and development. If a child is being baptised, it is the responsibility of the parents and godparents, with the support of the whole church, to ensure this continued growth. Adult candidates also need support in their growth in discipleship and faith.

Darkness and Light

He has rescued us from the power of darkness and transferred us into the kingdom of his beloved Son ... (Colossians 1:13)

In baptism, God calls us out of darkness into his marvellous light.
(From 'The Decision')

May Almighty God deliver you from the powers of darkness, restore in you the image of his glory and lead you in the light and obedience of Christ.
(From 'The Signing with the Cross')

Baptism is seen as calling from darkness to light. A lighted candle is given as a symbol of Christ, the light of the world. The symbolism of turning from an old way of life to a new one is prevalent in baptism liturgy. The candidates signal their intention to live a different way of life, going in a new direction with God. The candidates (or those speaking on their behalf) therefore make statements of decision to renounce evil and turn towards Christ. It is seen as a movement from darkness to light.

Washing

And baptism ... now saves you – not as a removal of dirt from the body, but as an appeal to God for a good conscience, through the resurrection of Jesus Christ ... (1 Peter 3:21)

Now sanctify this water that, by the power of the Holy Spirit, they may be cleansed from sin ... (From 'The Prayer over the Water')

Baptism is also a symbolic cleansing from sin with the water. The imagery of washing away' sin and guilt is a theme found throughout the Bible. It is an obvious image which has a clear resonance in everyday activity.

Dying and Rising

Therefore we have been buried with him by baptism into death, so that, just as Christ was raised from the dead by the glory of the Father, so we too might walk in newness of life. (Romans 6:4)

We thank you, Father for the water of baptism. In it we are buried with Christ in his death. By it we share in his resurrection.
(From 'The Prayer over the Water')

Echoing the death and resurrection of Christ, there is a strong theme of dying to the old self and rising to new life, which becomes all the more pointed if the candidate is fully immersed and is 'buried' in the water, only to rise up out of it again.

Being Clothed with Christ

As many of you as were baptised into Christ have clothed yourselves with Christ. (Galatians 3:27)

Here we are clothed with Christ, dying to sin that we may live his risen life.
(From 'The Introduction')

In early baptism practice, the candidates were often baptised naked and then clothed afterwards in white, as a sign of putting on the 'garment' of faith. Thankfully this doesn't happen today – the 'clothing' is now more symbolically expressed! Some people may wear white for their baptism as a sign of this clothing in Christ.

The Journey

In baptism, these children begin their journey in faith.
(From 'The Presentation of the Candidates')

In baptism God invites you on a life-long journey. Together with all God's people, you must explore the way of Jesus ... (From 'The Commission')

One of the primary themes of baptism is that of the Christian life as a journey in Christ. At baptism we begin this journey, joining with our fellow pilgrims on the way, including those who have gone before and those who will follow on.

BOOKS, ETC.

Buchanan, Colin, *A Case for Infant Baptism* (Nottingham: Grove Books Worship Series W20)

Earey, Mark and Myers, Gilly (eds), *Common Worship Today* (London: HarperCollins, 2001)

Green, Michael, *Baptism* (London: Hodder and Stoughton, 1999)

Stevenson, Kenneth, *The Mystery of Baptism* (Norwich: Canterbury Press, 1998)

World Council of Churches, *Baptism, Eucharist and Ministry* (Geneva: WCC, 1997)

TRAVELLING TOGETHER

Introduction (15mins)

Welcome and prayer.

Last Session's Challenge
Share your imagined conversation with your friend about baptism.

Aim of This Session
To look at how baptism/confirmation initiate us into the journey of Jesus' disciples.

Liturgy

(You will need to have a copy of the baptism liturgy available.)

Reflection (20mins)

- If you are confirmed, what did your confirmation mean to you?
- What connection is there in your mind between baptism and confirmation?
- What effect has being baptised and confirmed had upon your discipleship and view of the church?
- How has your understanding of baptism and confirmation disposed you towards church traditions which do not practise confirmation?

Bible Bit (20mins)

Galatians 3:26–29
(In this passage St Paul suggests that baptism brings the disciple into a new relationship with God for which the Jewish Law or Torah was a preparation. The theology emerges from the actions of the liturgy.)

- How does this passage shed light on the understanding of baptism/confirmation which you spoke of earlier?
- What does this passage suggest about the Christian community and discipleship?

- In what ways does this passage expand your view of the Church?

Share Spot (15mins)

Talk about the Share Spot resources for this session, which look at sacraments.

- How do you think the sacraments relate to holy living?
- What is it about sacraments that most enriches your discipleship?

Ponder Point (5mins)

What has this session clarified about your discipleship?

Prayer (5mins)

Challenge

- Find time this week to record what you have learned from this session.
- Look at your local church and think how, together and dispersed, you could live out your baptismal identity more faithfully. Write your suggestions down and bring them with you next time.

Share Spot Resources

Sacraments
JOHN THOMSON

Moments of mystery are part of most people's lives. Virtually everyone has some sort of spiritual experience, which often comes through something ordinary and material. People often speak of finding God in their gardens, or when awestruck by the wonder of a sunset or the passion of the sea. Lovers sense the glory of God in their adoration and parents in the gift of children. Whilst such experiences can lead to idolatry or pantheism, they need not do so. Indeed to deny the reality of such encounter points with God would undermine a central truth of Christianity, namely that God and the material are compatible. Jesus was God among us in the flesh. This is not to suggest that God is identical with the material order, as pantheism does, but to say that God can identify with the created order. Spirit and matter are not opposites. Indeed in some sense matter is simply spirit or energy in a particular form. God is not in the gaps, as older views of deism implied. God participates in creation without being swallowed up in creation, much akin to the analogy of mind and brain. The mind is not identical with the brain, but without the brain there is no mind. Co-inherence best describes this truth; they are together but not the same.

All of this is embraced in Anglican understandings of the sacraments. The word 'sacrament' comes from the Latin *sacramentum* meaning 'something devoted to sacred use'. In Roman times it referred to the giving of a pledge of loyalty by a lord to his servant with reciprocal expectations of service. This was used by Latin translators of the Greek liturgies to cover the meaning of the Greek word *mysterion* from which English gets the word 'mystery', but which in New Testament terms is closer to the English word 'secret' (Ephesians 1:9). In this sense sacrament or mystery is that purpose of God for salvation disclosed in the ministry of Jesus Christ. Christ, as Karl Rahner argued, is the primal or fundamental sacrament. Through his presence in his people as the body of Christ, the Church derivatively becomes sacramental. What we call sacraments are therefore 'visible words' (Augustine of Hippo) of this Gospel now embodied in the Church.

The Catechism defines sacraments as 'outward signs of inward spiritual grace' and in the arguments of the sixteenth century this definition was held to refer to the 'dominical' sacraments, that is those commanded explicitly by Jesus the Lord (or in Latin *Jesus Dominus*) in the Scriptural witness, i.e. Baptism and Holy Communion. This was in contrast to the Medieval Church which had settled upon seven sacraments: Baptism, Confirmation, Eucharist, Penance, Marriage, Ordination and Unction. The Reformers felt that only the dominical sacraments expressed the Gospel in all its fullness. They also avoided sacramentalising all of reality, since, though holding to a graced view of creation, a distinction was made between the sense that the Holy Spirit sustains and participates in creation and the understanding of the saving and sanctifying character of Gospel grace in the sacraments.

Anglicans therefore have generally held a 'high' view of the sacraments. Christ is 're-presented' in the sacraments, not to complete the work of salvation, but to mediate the life-giving power of that once-for-all event of his life, death and resurrection. Nevertheless, because of the terrible conflicts of the Reformation era, a general latitude about the precise meaning of the sacraments was held. Christ is really present in the sacramental event without definition being given. Hence, today, different understandings about this are present within the Anglican church. Some Anglicans would hold that the grace of the sacraments, properly celebrated, is irresistible. Hence God's permanent (indelible) mark of grace is upon the baptised infant child even of godless parents. Others would stress the condition of the recipients of the sacraments and suggest that this impedes or facilitates the exposure of the person to grace. Some would see salvation as the ongoing gracing of life through the sacraments (imparted righteousness), as Augustine of Hippo taught. Others would stress the gift of salvation as something given once and forever (imputed righteousness) to people upon confession of faith in the manner expressed by Martin Luther. Others would go further and stress the exemplary function of sacraments, showing us how Christ lived the Gospel and how we ought to have our lives patterned.

However Anglicans have not departed from the discipline of the pre-Reformation Church, namely, that because these are sacraments of the Gospel through the Church, celebrating them involves the presence of three elements; the material element (*res* or thing), the ritual words (*verba* or liturgical words) and the priest (authorised representative of the Church). Due to high infant mortality it was accepted that the last could, in emergency, be a lay person.

Whilst there remain considerable differences of conviction about the nature and activity of sacraments within the Church as a whole, and certainly within the Anglican church, a number of implications can be drawn from the sacramental practice of Christian worship. First, sacraments speak of the social character of human living. They belong to the Church, not simply to the individual, and they are to sustain God's new society rather than simply satisfy private perceptions of spirituality. Furthermore, their social character points forward to the universal destiny of creation anticipated in the mixed bag of the Church gathered today. Second, they act as a sign of subversion, challenging all human pretensions to control creation or to represent evil and darkness as the victors in the cosmic clash between light and darkness. They represent God's global reign as real. Hence, in the face of oppression and powerlessness, sacraments both sustain and offer signs of hope. They materialise the protest of prayer. Third, sacraments imply ecological sensitivity. The offering of the material for the mediation of grace implies a hallowing of creation. It is God's gift and it remains God's. Hence our use of creation should attend to the character of the God whose gift mediates his life to his Church.

BOOKS, ETC,

Bradshaw, Tim, *The Olive Branch: An Evangelical Doctrine of the Church* (Carlisle: Paternoster Press, 1992), chapter 4 section 4

Francis, Mark R., 'Sacramental Theology' in Alister E. McGrath (ed.), *The Blackwell Encyclopaedia of Modern Christian Thought* (Oxford: Blackwell, 1993)

Jenson, Robert W., 'The Church and the Sacraments' in Colin E. Gunton (ed.), *The Cambridge Companion to Christian Doctrine* (Cambridge: CUP, 1999), pp. 207–25

McGrath, Alister E., *Christian Theology: An Introduction* (Oxford: Blackwell, 1995), chapter 14

McGrath, Alister E. (ed.), *The Christian Theology Reader* (Oxford: Blackwell, 1995), chapter 8

Richardson, Alan (ed.), *A Dictionary of Christian Theology* (London: SCM, London, 1982)

Williams, Rowan, *On Christian Theology* (Oxford: Blackwell, 2000), part 4

'YES, MINISTER!'

Introduction (15mins)

Welcome and prayer.

Last Session's Challenge

Share your thoughts on how your church might better display its baptismal identity.

Aims of This Session

To explore baptism-confirmation as a call to discipleship and ministry.

Liturgy

The symbolism of being signed and anointed in baptism-confirmation.

Reflection (20mins)

- What does being signed with the cross and anointed with oil at baptism-confirmation mean to you?
- What, if any, connections are there in your mind between discipleship, ministry and this experience?
- Divide a large piece of paper into two sections. List as many different uses of the word 'minister' as you can think of on one side of the paper and on the other side, list as many 'ministries' as you can think of which are exercised in your local church.
- What connections, if any, are there between your two lists?

Bible Bit (20mins)

1 Corinthians 12
(This passage is at the heart of St Paul's understanding of being church as properly being like a healthy human body. The fractious Corinthian church were far from this vision of a healthy church.)

- How does Paul's picture link baptism and ministry?
- What are Paul's principal convictions about the church and the character of its ministry?
- How does your church's practice of ministry (written on the paper) relate to St Paul's image of the body?
- What areas of service need attention in your church and local community?
- How does your understanding of confirmation relate to this?

Share Spot (15mins)

Talk about the Share Spot resources for this session, which look at ministry development opportunities.

- What does it mean for you to serve the strangers in your neighbourhood?
- How could you share in the Church's life, ministry and mission more effectively?

Ponder Point (5mins)

What has this session clarified about your discipleship?

Prayer (5mins)

Challenge

- Find time this week to record what you have learned from this session.
- Using the SWOT analysis method (Strengths, Weaknesses, Opportunities and Threats) evaluate the state of your church's ministry as an expression of the body of Christ in your local context. Then do the same for your own life, as an ambassador for this body in daily living.

Share Spot Resources

Discipleship, Strangers and the Image of God
IAN McCOLLOUGH

As Christians, we are constantly challenged by our own claim to be disciples of Jesus. The challenges we face are those he lived out in his teaching and his befriending of those considered outside the generally accepted orthodox system in the manner in which it was implemented, but fully expressed in the Scriptures he knew.

In his book *The Dignity of Difference* the Chief Rabbi, Sir Jonathan Sacks, quotes an ancient Jewish teaching: 'When a human being makes many coins in the same mint, they all come out the same. God makes every person in the same image, his image, and each is different.' Each is valued and irreplaceable to God. Jonathan Sacks states that in the Hebrew Bible there are no fewer than 36 commands to 'love the stranger':

> You shall not oppress a stranger, for you know the heart of the stranger. You yourselves were strangers in the land of Egypt. (Exodus 23:9)

> When a stranger lives with you in your land, do not ill-treat him. The stranger who lives with you shall be treated like the native-born. Love him as yourself, for you were strangers in the land of Egypt. I am the Lord your God.
> (Leviticus 19:33–4)

Jesus lived and acted out the teachings he received and spoke to his time and culture as a Jew. As Christians we believe his teaching and example are relevant for all time. The Gospel readings reveal Jesus' commitment to indicating God's preferred way for individuals and institutions through his teaching and in his engaging with the stranger either as Gentile (Matthew 15:21–28; Mark 7:24–30), woman (Luke 7:36–50), children (Mark 10:13–16), diseased people (Luke 17:11–19), an 'unclean' woman (Matthew 9:20–22; Mark 5:24–34; Luke 8:43–48), an 'enemy' (Matthew 8:5–13; Luke 7:1–10), or a religious outsider (John 4:7–26).

In the parable of the Good Samaritan (Luke 10:25–37), Jesus showed that the actions of the stranger in meeting the needs of others were acceptable to God. The Jesus we follow challenges our tribal attitudes and behaviour and as Christians we believe the challenge is to people of all faiths and none for tolerance and welcome. While as a faith group we have not shared the history of the Jewish people, we have all been strangers at some times in our lives. Equally, we remember the pain of the times when we have been frozen out and excluded as being an outsider.

Much of the fear we have about other individuals and groups is based on our lack of knowledge of them or their customs. However, as human beings, we share with them all the same hopes and fears for our families and ourselves for good health, to be happy and to reach our full potential. The change in our attitude comes through those who, being strangers to us and us to them, have made us welcome, sometimes inviting us into their circle of friends and even their family. Through their specific act we have seen them in a new light.

The challenge to the religious imagination is to see God's image in one who is not in our image – the stranger, the one who is not like us. It will not be easy, but we could start by accepting that we are all made in God's image and that our differences tells us something about the greatness of God. It challenges all our narrow-minded attitudes and questions whether our preference for the familiar is really of God. How many of our contacts are with people we have met recently or are getting to know?

Under our growing awareness of the God who has created each of us, we are each asked to allow others into our lives, to encourage mutual growth and the wider contribution as part of the world family. These steps are necessary for the creation of a safer world, remembering that a house that is divided cannot stand. It will affect how we respond to situations where others would have us believe that their exclusive behaviour is acceptable. The actions and attitudes we present to others tell them more about our image of God than our words and creeds will ever say. Our discipleship and that of our churches must increasingly reflect the Jesus we follow if we expect to influence our neighbours.

BOOKS, ETC.

Alison, James, *Knowing Jesus* (London: SPCK, 1998)
Green, Laurie, *Urban Ministry and the Kingdom of God* (London: SPCK, 2003)
Hauerwas, Stanley, and Willimon, William H., *Where Resident Aliens Live: Exercises for Christian Practices* (Nashville: Abingdon Press, 1996)
—*The Truth About God: The Ten Commandments in Christian Life* (Nashville: Abingdon Press, 1999)
Hauerwas, Stanley, and Willimon, William H., with Saye, Scott C., *Lord, Teach Us: The Lord's Prayer and the Christian Life* (Nashville: Abingdon Press, 1996)
Lofink, G., *Jesus and Community: The Social Dimension of Christian Faith* (London: SPCK, 1985)
Sacks, Jonathan, *The Dignity of Difference* (London: Continuum, 2003)
Thomson, John B., *Church on Edge: Practising Christian Ministry Today* (London: Darton, Longman and Todd, 2004)

Ministry and Synods
GORDON TAYLOR

The world-wide Church is the body of Christ, commissioned to do God's work in the world by the power of the Holy Spirit. The Church of England is part of that body, with a particular calling to witness to and to serve the English nation and its local communities.

In the Anglican tradition authority is to be found in leadership by bishops, combined with government by Synods, representing bishops, clergy and lay people. In other words, leadership is by bishops but with consultation and consent.

A Synod is a Church assembly, a gathering of representatives of the members of the Church, to make decisions for the life, worship, work and witness of the Church.

In the Church of England, since 1970, there have been three tiers of synods, the General Synod, Diocesan Synod and Deanery Synod. In the General Synod and Diocesan Synod, bishops, clergy and laity are present together, but in Deanery Synods there are only the clergy and representatives of the lay people from the parishes of the deanery.

The General Synod is the national governing body of the Church of England. It makes laws for the Church, and is a forum where the Church can debate important national issues. It has 480 members and meets at least twice each year, in London and in York. The Archbishop of Canterbury and the Archbishop of York are joint Presidents of the Synod. The General Synod is made up of three Houses – the House of Bishops, the House of Clergy and the House of Laity. All diocesan bishops are members of the House of Bishops, along with some elected suffragan bishops. The House of Clergy is made up of representative deans, archdeacons, some others and clergy from each diocese, elected by the House of Clergy in the dioceses. The House of Laity consists of representatives for each diocese elected by the lay members of each Deanery Synod, some others, and a few *ex officio* members. Elections are held every five years.

The Diocesan Synod is the governing body of the diocese and is presided over by the diocesan bishop. This Synod considers matters concerning the Church of England and makes provision for them in relation to the diocese. It advises the bishop on any matter on which he may consult the Synod and it deals with matters referred to it by the General Synod as well as the financing of the diocese. It sets up various boards and committees which initiate and co-ordinate much of the Church's work throughout the diocese. Its members, both clerical and lay, are elected by the Deanery Synods, along with some *ex officio* members, and some nominated by the bishop. Elections are held every three years.

Each deanery also has a Synod, which consists of all the clergy serving in a deanery, along with elected lay representatives from each parish in the deanery. It considers matters referred to it from the Diocesan Synod and can raise matters for discussion at the Diocesan Synod, which gives access all the way to the General Synod. The Deanery Synod is also an appropriate place for local clergy and lay people to join together in worship, fellowship, discussion and mission. The Deanery Synod brings together the views of the parishes of the deanery, encourages a sense of community and interdependence amongst the parishes and promotes in the deanery the whole mission of the Church, evangelistic, social and ecumenical. Its lay members are elected every three years.

BOOKS, ETC.

Behrens, James, *Practical Church Management: A Guide for every Parish* (Leominster: Gracewing, 1998)

Dudley, Martin and Rounding, Virginia, *The Parish Survival Guide* (London: SPCK, 2004)

MacMorran, Kenneth M. and Briden, Timothy J., *A Handbook for Churchwardens and Church Councillors* (London: Mowbray, 1997)

Pritchford, John, *An ABC for the PCC: A Handbook for Church Council Members* (London: Continuum, 2000)

Synodical Government in the Church of England: A Review (London: Church House Publishing, 1997)

LITURGY OF THE SACRAMENTS:
THE EUCHARIST

THANKSGIVING

Introduction (15mins)

Welcome and prayer.

Last Session's Challenge

Share the results of your SWOT analysis of your church's ministry.

Aim of This Session

To explore the meaning of giving thanks (Eucharist).

Liturgy

The Liturgy of the Sacrament

The peace of the Lord be always with you;
and also with you.

Yours, Lord, is the greatness, the power,
the glory, the splendour and the majesty;
for everything in heaven and on earth is yours.
All things come from you,
and of your own do we give you.

The Lord is here.
His Spirit is with us.
Lift up your hearts.
We lift them to the Lord.
Let us give thanks to the Lord our God.
It is right to give thanks and praise.
(Prayer of Thanksgiving)

Reflection (20mins)

Think about the Peace.

- What happens in your church when the Peace is said?
- What do you think the Peace is about?
- How does the sign of the Peace suggest an agenda for Christian living?

Think about the Offertory *(when money, bread and wine are offered to God)*.

- What do you think the Offertory is all about?
- How does your church's stewardship speak of this sort of offering?

Think about the Thanksgiving *(the remainder of the prayer)*.

- What is your understanding of this prayer?
- What might it mean for a church to be a Eucharistic community?

Bible Bit (30mins)

Ephesians 1:3–14
(In this passage the blessings of God's salvation cascade from the pen, setting the context for the vision of church life that follows.)

On one side of a large piece of paper, write down the main features of this passage. Then do the same for one of the Eucharistic prayers (from *The Book of Common Prayer* or *Common Worship*).

- What comparisons can you make?
- How does this relate to your thoughts on the Peace, the Offertory and the Thanksgiving?
- From this, can you suggest how Christians can live thanksgiving in a suffering world?

Share Spot (15mins)

Talk about the Share Spot resources for this session, which look at living graciously as a Eucharistic community.

- What do you think is the relationship between the Eucharist and Christian giving?
- What regeneration challenges face your community and how might the church share graciously with that community?

Ponder Point (5mins)

What has this session clarified about your discipleship?

Prayer (5mins)

Challenge

* Find time this week to record what you have learned from this session.
* Compare and contrast the way Comic Relief goes about getting people to give with how your church goes about it. What, if anything, is different about Christian giving?
* Prepare for the next meeting by going through the next session.

Share Spot Resources

Christian Giving
NICK HUTTON

Money is a word that many people in church find difficult or embarrassing to use. This is odd because Jesus spoke about money and our relationship to it more than anything else. He understood that our relationship with money defines us as human beings.

Money is not a good or a bad thing in itself. Money is neutral. From 1 Timothy 6:10 we learn that it is the love of money which is the root of all kinds of evil, not money itself. Money, after all, is one of the many assets we are given by God. Like all these gifts – our talents, our skills, our ability to make things and create great works of art, and everything else we can think of that is wonderful about the world – money has been granted us to use for good or evil. Christians believe that we have that choice, and we are taught to be good stewards of our money to help to further God's kingdom in this world.

If we are active members of a caring charity, we expect to use our money to help further that charity's interests. For some reason, many people can be active church members without feeling that they have to commit their money to the church to enable its work.

In the past, it used to be argued that Christians should be persuaded to give by explaining to them the intricacies of church finances. For example, in the Church of England it is certainly good to understand the importance of the inter-relationships between parishes and that wealthier parishes should support not only their own ministry but also that of churches in difficult inner-city areas. It is also important for there to be an understanding that the Parish Share (Quota) is not a tax but a fair way of raising the resources to provide for the costs of our clergy.

However, these are not the reasons Christians are asked to commit a proportion of our income to our church. Christian giving is about having a clear vision of what

God wants us to do in our parish or district, and then using the gifts we, as individuals, have been given by him, in thankfulness.

'All things come from you, and of your own do we give you.' God gives us everything we have, and we have a need to give him something of our riches back. If we are ungenerous in our giving, we show that we cannot think much of God. We are told in Matthew 6, 'Where your money is, there is your heart also.'

Jesus says, 'Do you understand what I have done for you?' (John13:12). Our giving is a measure of our response to that. To give willingly and happily is a large part of the joy of being a Christian. It is part of the Christian package. If we want to see our faith carried out in practice, it must be resourced. That can happen only if Christians, the body of the church, will it and make it happen by expressing our faith by our giving.

BOOKS, ETC

Halfpenny, Peter, *Individual Giving and Volunteering in Britain: Who Gives What ... and Why?* 5th edn (Tonbridge: CAF, 1991)

Mann, Adrian, Stevens, Robin and Willmington, John, *First Fruits: A Worship Anthology on Generosity and Giving* (Norwich: Canterbury Press, 2001)

Morris, E., *Receiving and Giving: The Basic Issues and Implications of Christian Giving* (London: Central Board of Finance of the Church of England, 1990)

Swinson, Antonia, *Root of All Evil: How to Make Spiritual Values Count* (Edinburgh: St Andrew Press, 2003)

Wright, Michael, *Yours Lord: A Handbook of Christian Stewardship* (London: Mowbray, 1992)

Christianity and Regeneration
MICHAEL WAGSTAFF

Most people in our age associate regeneration with the rebuilding and revitalising of urban communities. It is a process that stems from economic need and political will, and it is something that the Church has been an enthusiastic partner to in many communities. Churches open their doors to local groups and the Church becomes a player and a partner in local initiatives by sharing its physical and human resources.

But this really can only be an *outcome* of the process of regeneration. Regeneration begins in the Gospel, with a Jesus who relates to the people around him not only by preaching, but more essentially by listening. And it is when people tell him their story and their needs that he can heal and turn around lives.

The Jesus who prays and studies in the synagogue but who lives out his faith in the towns and the villages and on the road is a Jesus who has been lost to many Christians. Too many of us expect people to *come to church* and see the whole of the work of salvation happening there. It is only when we follow Jesus to encounter people, their stories and their needs, that we are going to be able to begin to respond to their needs. And if we are to do that, we have to accept that a church that seeks to regenerate its community is a church that undergoes itself a true process of regeneration.

The first transforming power of regeneration lies in *generosity*. A worshipping community has to risk giving what it has to the community, with the faith that some things will be lost in order for many more things to be gained. You may lose something of your much-loved church interior. You may have the peace of your tradition disturbed. But that is the price to pay for entertaining angels unawares. We never lose anything if we are prepared to share.

The second lies in a new-found wealth of experience to be found in a community that increasingly turns its back on the Church. This is not about *bums on pews* but about Christians finding new understanding of the life of the community God calls us to serve. And through that understanding comes mission. Jesus would never have found his apostles and disciples if he had waited around in the synagogue for them to turn up, but they were the very ones who took the Gospel to the world.

Regeneration will also allow people to discover great gifts in themselves. Looking at the community to produce a social audit, forming management and policy teams in equal and productive partnership with individuals and organisations in the community give people the chance to grow in confidence and ability. Having life in abundance is about knowing your gifts and your potential – that knowledge regenerates people.

If the Church is a partner in rebuilding and revitalising communities, it will learn to rebuild and revitalise itself. It will get to know its neighbours – the people God has called every Christian man and woman to serve. It is not an easy process, and requires great courage and a lot of hard work. But the alternative is decay, or even degeneration.

BOOKS, ETC.

Farnell, Richard *et al.*, *Faith in Urban Regeneration? Engaging Faith Communities in Urban Regeneration* (Bristol: Policy Press, 2003)

Green, Laurie, *Urban Ministry and the Kingdom of God* (London: SPCK, 2003)

Grundy, Malcolm, *Community Work: A Handbook for Volunteer Groups and Local Churches* (London: Mowbray, 1995)

Ward, Graham, *Cities of God* (London: Routledge, 2000)

MEMORY AND MEALS

Introduction (15mins)

Welcome and prayer.

Last Session's Challenge
Share your insights on Christian giving.

Aim of This Session
To explore the place of memory and meals in discipleship.

Liturgy

Who, in the same night that he was betrayed,
took bread and gave you thanks;
he broke it and gave it to his disciples, saying:
Take, eat; this is my body which is given for you;
do this in remembrance of me.

In the same way, after supper
he took the cup and gave you thanks;
he gave it to them, saying:
Drink this, all of you:
this is my blood of the new covenant,
which is shed for you and for many for the forgiveness of sins.
Do this, as often as you drink it,
in remembrance of me.

Reflection (20mins)

- What does 'Do this ... in remembrance of me' mean for you as you share in the Eucharist?
- How do your church building and graveyard (if you have one) enrich this remembering?

- What does the practice of eating together at the Eucharist mean for your understanding of Christian living?

Bible Bit (20mins)

Compare the different accounts of the Last Supper (Matthew 26:20–29; Mark 14:22–25; Luke 22:14–23 and 1 Corinthians 11:23–26).

- Discuss how and why you think these accounts have their own distinctiveness.
- How do they shed light on your thinking about memory and meals in Christian discipleship?
- Assuming that the background to this meal is the Passover (cf. Exodus 12), how might this inform the way we understand the Eucharist?

Notice the fourfold action performed by Jesus. He *takes* the bread, he *blesses* and gives thanks for the bread, he *breaks* the bread, he *shares* the bread.

- In what way might this be a pattern for the life of the church, as Jesus' disciples in the world?
- Do your reflections add anything to what you were sharing earlier?

Share Spot (15mins)

Talk about the Share Spot resources for this session, which look at the history of the Eucharist and its themes.

- How do you feel about the history of the Eucharist?
- Which of the themes in the Eucharist matter most to you and why?
- How might the Seder meal shed light on the meaning of the Eucharist?

Ponder Point (5mins)

What has this session clarified about your discipleship?

Prayer (5mins)

Challenge

- Find time this week to record what you have learned from this session.
- As a group prepare a Passover meal using the *Celebration of Redemption* Seder Meal Pack. Details of how to obtain this pack can be found in the Introduction: Facilitator's Notes. Begin the next session by telling the story which this meal embodies as you eat the food. Imagine what this feels like if you are Jewish.

• Prepare for the next meeting by going through the next session.

Share Spot Resources

The Eucharist
EMMA INESON

1. HISTORY

Over time, the celebration of Holy Communion has changed and been argued about, both in its practical enactment and its theological understanding. We bring this heritage to our Communion tables today.

The Eucharist in the Bible

For the Jewish people, meals had always been sacred events, re-enacting truths about God. In the last meal Christ shared with his friends, at Passover, they too enacted the history of the Jewish people, remembering that God had protected them in the land of Egypt, delivered them from slavery and fed them in the wilderness. At this meal, Jesus linked the bread of life with his own body, which was to be broken on the cross, and the wine (recalling the blood of the lambs daubed on the doorposts of the Israelites in Egypt) with his own blood, which would deliver humanity. Every time a Eucharist is celebrated, the participants fulfil the instruction of Christ, when he broke the bread of his body and blessed the wine of his blood and said: 'Do this in remembrance of me' (Luke 22:19).

The Eucharist in the Middle Ages

For the earliest Christians, the Eucharist still took the form of a full, shared meal, with accompanying liturgy. One of the earliest writings about a Eucharistic meal is Justin Martyr's *First Apology* (AD 150). A Eucharistic meal would have included readings, a homily and prayers, especially a thanksgiving prayer over the bread and wine. By the time Hippolytus was writing his *Apostolic Tradition* (AD 215) the Eucharist had lost some of the similarities to a meal. Only bread and wine were consumed, and the whole thing had become more ritualised.

Over the following centuries, the celebration of the Eucharistic meal changed dramatically. The sense of mystery surrounding the sacraments increased. The actual elements (the bread and the wine) became more and more venerated as the doctrine of transubstantiation (the belief that the bread and wine actually became the body and blood of Christ) gained more credence. The liturgy was said in Latin and lay people received communion less frequently (often only at Easter). They weren't allowed to take the wine in case they spilt it. For lay people, the Eucharist (or Mass) was a chance for them to 'witness the miracle', rather than actually to receive the bread and wine. In the Middle Ages, it became common for a Mass to be said to reduce the time a soul was believed to spend in purgatory. It was to all these changes that the Reformers objected, especially to the sense that grace was becoming a commodity to be purchased by the rich, who paid for priests to say Mass for their souls.

The Eucharist and the Reformation

The main contention of the Reformation was what *exactly* Christ meant when he said, 'This is my body' and 'This is my blood' and *how* the bread and the wine represented Christ's sacrifice at the Eucharistic celebration.

Luther, Calvin, Cranmer and the Council of Trent (Roman Catholics) believed in the 'real presence' of Christ in the elements, but in different ways. For Luther, the presence of Jesus joined the bread and wine but did not change their character (Consubstantiation). For Calvin, the Holy Spirit made real the presence of Jesus as the believer received in faith the elements (Receptionism). For the Council of Trent, the appearance of bread and wine remained the same but their substance was changed into the body of Christ (Transubstantiation). For Cranmer the key was being invited to share in the heavenly banquet made real by the Holy Spirit (Ascensionism). For Zwingli, the bread and wine were simply signs, pointing the believer to the spiritual benefits of what Jesus had done on the cross (Nominalism). For none was Jesus' sacrifice repeated, although the Roman Catholics believed that the Mass was a re-presenting of the sacrifice of Calvary and was the means by which its grace was made available to the believer. For the Reformers, this undermined the 'once for all' character of Calvary – its benefits were to be received by faith rather than by going to Mass as often as possible.

The Eucharist in the Modern Period

Since the Reformers, the practice and understanding of the Eucharist have gone through changes, although none causing such drastic consequences as the Reformation. For the Church of England *The Book of Common Prayer* of 1662 continues to be the standard in form and doctrine. In the nineteenth century, the Oxford Movement advocated a return to a more Roman Catholic understanding of the sacraments and a more ceremonial approach to the liturgy. In the early twentieth century the Parish and People movement (which had as its slogan 'The Lord's Service for the Lord's People on the Lord's Day') aimed to make the Eucharist more accessible to more people more often. Currently, a major topic of discussion and development in Eucharistic thinking is the increased opportunity for the admission of children to Communion before Confirmation. Liturgically speaking, the introduction of *Common Worship* has been a recent, major change in the Church of England.

2. THE SHAPE OF THE EUCHARIST

The earliest Eucharistic liturgies take a shape that starts with a greeting, readings and a sermon (the Ministry of the Word), goes on to include prayers and then ends in a shared meal (the Ministry of the Sacrament). Our modern Communion services take a similar structure. In 1945, Dom Gregory Dix wrote an important book called *The Shape of the Liturgy*, which highlights the pattern of Jesus' celebration at the Last Supper. The shape of the present-day Eucharistic prayer reflects this pattern where we:

1. take bread and wine,
2. give thanks for the bread and wine,
3. break the bread and
4. share the bread and wine.

3. THEMES IN THE EUCHARIST

Feeding

> Eat and drink in remembrance that he died for you, and feed on him in your hearts by faith with thanksgiving.
>
> (*Common Worship* Order One, prayer before the Giving of Communion)

Holy Communion has always been thought of in terms of a meal, at which people eat together. But what is it that we feed on? What did Jesus mean when he said, 'This is my body' (Matthew 26:26 and echoed in liturgy through the ages)? The question of whether and how Christ is represented in the bread and wine at the Eucharist has been the subject of the biggest debate in the history of the church, as we have seen. However it is understood, the sacrament of Holy Communion remains the most significant meeting place between God and his people, and provides a strengthening and equipping for service.

Remembering

> This is our story.
> **This is our song.**
>
> (*Common Worship* Order One, Eucharistic Prayer D)

For any community, remembering our story is what gives us a common heritage and binds us together. In the Eucharist Christian communities remember and re-enact the story of God and his people, and most significantly, the story of the death and resurrection of Jesus Christ. It sets our worship in the context and history of worship throughout the ages.

Thanksgiving

> Let us give thanks to the Lord our God.
> **It is right to give thanks and praise.**
>
> (*Common Worship* Order One)

The word Eucharist means simply 'thanksgiving'. One of the things we do at the Lord's Table is to give thanks for what he has done for humanity in the cross of Christ. The 'offering' of our thanks and praise echoes and responds to the sacrifice made for us on the cross.

Sharing

> We break this bread
> to share in the body of Christ.
> **Though we are many, we are one body,**
> **because we all share in one bread.**
>> (*Common Worship* Order One, Prayer at the Breaking of the Bread)

During Holy Communion, the bond between the fellowship of believers is strengthened. As we 'share in the body of Christ' we are aware that there is another meaning of 'the body of Christ' – the Church. This sharing also makes us mindful of the Church throughout the world and throughout history.

Looking Forward

> ... we celebrate his resurrection, his bursting from the tomb ...
> and we long for his coming in glory.
>> (*Common Worship* Order One, Eucharistic Prayer F)

Early Communion accounts, especially the *Didache* (AD 60–120), had a highly eschatological flavour. The Eucharist not only looks back and remembers, but also looks forward and anticipates the Lord's return when the feasting will be heavenly.

4. THE EUCHARIST AND THE WORLD

It might seem obvious to state that after the Eucharist, we leave! This going out into the world is, in a sense, a crucial part of the celebration. When we have been fed by the bread and the wine, received God's grace, remembered our history, shared fellowship and glimpsed a taste of heaven, our mission and our task is to go and share these things with the wider world.

> **May we who share Christ's body live his risen life;**
> **we who drink his cup bring life to others;**
> **we whom the Spirit lights give light to the world.**
>> (*Common Worship* Order One, Prayer after Communion)

BOOKS, ETC.

Buchanan, Colin and Read, Charles, *The Eucharistic Prayers of Order One* (Nottingham: Grove Books Worship Series W158, 2001)

Fletcher, Jeremy, *Communion in Common Worship* (Nottingham: Grove Books Worship Series W159, 2000)

Holeton, David, *Renewing the Anglican Eucharist* (Cambridge: Grove Booklets, 1996)

McPartlan, Paul, *Sacrament of Salvation: An Introduction to Eucharistic Ecclesiology* (Edinburgh: T. & T. Clark, 1995)

Perham, Michael, *Lively Sacrifice: Eucharist in the Church of England Today* (London: SPCK, 1992)

Ward, Pete (ed.), *Mass Culture* (Oxford: Bible Reading Fellowship, 1999)

Welker, Michael, *What Happens in Holy Communion* (London: SPCK, 2000)

World Council of Churches, *Baptism, Eucharist and Ministry* (Geneva: WCC, 1997)

Wright, Tom, *Holy Communion for Amateurs* (London: Hodder and Stoughton, 1999)

COMMUNITY AND CREATION

Introduction

Welcome and prayer.

Last Session's Challenge

Share the Seder meal you have prepared. (Decide your own timings.)

Aim of This Session

To explore the relationship between Eucharist, community and creation.

Liturgy

Accept through him, our great high priest,
this our sacrifice of thanks and praise,
and as we eat and drink these holy gifts
in the presence of your divine majesty,
renew us by your Spirit,
inspire us with your love
and unite us in the body of your Son,
Jesus Christ our Lord.

Through him and with him and in him,
in the unity of the Holy Spirit,
with all who stand before you in earth and heaven,
we worship you, Father almighty,
in songs of everlasting praise.
Blessing and honour and glory and power
Be yours for ever and ever.
Amen.

The Lord's Prayer

Our Father in heaven,
hallowed be your name,

your kingdom come,
your will be done,
on earth as in heaven.
Give us today our daily bread.
Forgive us our sins
as we forgive those who sin against us.
Lead us not into temptation,
but deliver us from evil.
For the kingdom, the power,
and the glory are yours
now and for ever.
Amen.

The Breaking of the Bread

We break this bread
to share in the body of Christ.
**Though we are many, we are one body,
because we all share in one bread.**

Reflection (20mins)

Reflect upon the meal you have just shared and the liturgy above:

* What sort of Christian community is God calling us to become?
* How does your church express this sort of community?
* Share your understanding about the symbolism of the bread and wine.
* How does the Eucharist inform our understanding of creation?
* Are there any particular ways in which your church witnesses to nature being God's creation?

Bible Bit (20mins)

Compare Genesis 1, John 1:1–18 and Revelation 21.
(These three passages are about creation, Christ and community.)

* How do these passages shed light on your answers to the questions you have just engaged in?

Share Spot (15mins)

Talk about the Share Spot resources for this session, which suggest how Christians might relate to the challenges creation presents to a Eucharistic Christian community.

- Which creation challenge reflected upon in the Share Spot resources engaged you most and why?
- How do you think the church should explore such challenges?

Ponder Point (5mins)

What has this session clarified about your discipleship?

Prayer (5mins)

Challenge

- Find time this week to record what you have learned from this session.
- Set yourself a challenge to live more respectfully of creation, e.g. your modes of transport, your use of energy, recycling rubbish, etc.
- At the next session bring a resolution expressing how your life must change if you are to live out this dimension of the Eucharist.
- Prepare for the next meeting by going through the next session.

Share Spot Resources

Christianity and Disability
DAVID BLISS

St Paul says: 'The body does not consist of one member but of many. If the foot should say, "Because I am not a hand, I do not belong to the body ..."' (1 Corinthians 12:14–15ff). This is a reminder that the body of Christ, the Church, is made of many different parts and those different parts include people with different disabilities. Luke reminds us of the ministry of Jesus as he records the occasion when Jesus read in the synagogue: 'He has sent me to proclaim release to the captives and recovering of sight to the blind' (Luke 4:18). Jesus later replied to John's messengers: 'Go and tell John what you have seen and heard: the blind receive their sight, the lame walk, lepers are cleansed, and the deaf hear' (Luke 7:22). At the heart of the ministry of Jesus was the disabled person. Therefore the work and ministry of the church must also focus on the disabled. The disabled face many obstacles in ordinary everyday life – the message of the Gospel compels us to do all that we can to remove the obstacles that may hinder their worship and relationship with Christ.

The question of disability should be very much at the forefront of discussion within our churches today. From a practical point many churches, particularly older ones, were not designed with disabilities in mind. Large pillars, for example, make for both visual and aural difficulties and steps create problems for wheelchairs.

Many other areas could also be looked at to ensure that those with disabilities are not in some way excluded from or hindered in their worship. It would be a good exercise for all churches to conduct a Disability Audit similar to the one contained in *Widening the Eye of the Needle*.

BOOKS, ETC.

Penton, John, *Widening the Eye of the Needle: Access to Church Buildings for People with Disabilities* (London: Church House Publishing, 1995)

'The Church among Deaf People', Advisory Board of Ministry, Ministry Paper No. 14 (GS1247) (London: Church House Publishing, 1997)

Christianity and Development
JOHN THOMSON

From its earliest roots, Christianity has been involved in what can be described as 'development'. From baptism, the challenge to Christians is to grow up into the maturity of Christ, a challenge which has been interpreted in many ways, socially, educationally, medically and creatively. Equally the commitment, inherited from Judaism, to love our neighbour ensured that expressions of human development were not limited to the Christian community alone.

More modern notions of development, however, represent an ambiguous relationship with this tradition. In part the technological development of western societies, together with its social and military implications, has enabled this tradition to become dominant in world affairs for the past two or three centuries. This has given the impression that development is about becoming like western societies (sometimes called the North), a notion increasingly reacted against by representatives of other parts of the world. The western Christian church in some sense colluded with this in the nineteenth and twentieth centuries, as many missionaries uncritically equated Christianity with other western ideals and practices. Hence people in what is called 'the South' are increasingly asking 'development in terms of who and what?'

In response to this reaction, notions of development have come to be seen as about empowering people where they are with the resources to develop in ways which respect their traditions and identities. This does not mean that local perspectives are not held accountable, but rather that consultation and attention to particular communities is felt to be a better approach than imposing abstract views of development originating in very different societies.

Development is therefore a contested notion. Christians, however, are well positioned to make a contribution here, since the churches represent a global conversational community in a way often difficult for other agencies, governments, the United Nations or charities to emulate. Conversation includes a mixture of listening, recognising historical legacies such as colonialism, and seeking a way forward in a respectful and recognisably responsible way. Recent campaigns, such as the Debt Relief Jubilee 2000 campaign, the Fair Trade project and Make Poverty History, are examples of such conversations.

BOOKS, ETC.

Allen, T. and Thomas, A., *Poverty and Development into the 21st Century* (Oxford: OUP, 2000)

Banking on the Poor: The Ethics of Third World Debt (London: Christian Aid, 1988)

Bilton, T. *et al.*, *Introductory Sociology* (London: Macmillan Press, 1997)

Fenn-Tye, Kate (ed.), *Voices from the South* (Dunblane: Action of Churches Together in Scotland, 2004)

Madden, Peter, *A Raw Deal: Trade and the World's Poor*, 2nd edn (London: Christian Aid, 1992)

Reed, Charles, *Development Matters: Christian Perspectives on Globalisation* (London: Church House Publishing, 2001)

Web sites: Christian Aid, Tear Fund, CAFOD, Oxfam, World Bank, PovertNet, United Nations, CIA profiles, Dfid (Department for International Development, UK).

Christianity and Gender
JOHN THOMSON

Gender is popularly understood to represent the female and male sexual forms of animals and plants. However with the rise of the natural sciences, medicine and psychology distinctions have been made between 'sex' meaning the biological differences of male and female, 'sexuality', meaning how a person understands their sexual orientation, and 'gender' meaning sexual identity as a social construction, i.e. how sexual roles, etc. are formed through social expectations. In addition, a greater awareness of the fluidity of identity has challenged notions of fixed and atomistic views of personhood, sexual identity and role. Biology is no longer seen as determining identity and role.

All of this has raised challenging questions for ancient religions, not least Christianity, whose formative texts and traditions emerged long before such insights were available. In consequence, some Christians believe that these modern notions go beyond the bounds of acceptable Christian ethics. For Anglicans, as in the nineteenth-century debates about creation and evolution, the question involves the relationship between Scripture, tradition and reason (understood as sound learning).

Having noted this, it is clear that even in the biblical tradition, questions of the way sex, sexuality and gender are conceived are more flexible than is sometimes recognised. Genesis 1:26 was a challenge to ancient views of God as either male or female. In the Gospels we read of Jesus, a male rabbi, relating to a variety of women, sometimes in apparently ambiguous contexts (John 4). The birth of Jesus places a young peasant woman in a life-threatening situation as sanctions against illegitimacy are threatened. The early church struggled as baptism suggested a vision of discipleship which took no account of gender distinctions. In addition, the Jewish roots of Christianity predisposed the church to concur with what modern feminists would call 'patriarchal' structures of society.

As Christianity spread across the eastern and western fringes of the Mediterranean, cultural practices informed the way in which male and female were understood within and beyond the church. Whilst the rise in celibacy drew some of its energy both from the practice of Jesus and from the primacy of the church as opposed to the biological family, it also reflected the ambiguity with which reproductive sexual practices were regarded. Reproduction for women was a life-threatening experience from which celibacy could be a liberation. For men large families could mean social significance, yet also high economic cost. Nevertheless the gender-equalising effects of celibacy were something of a threat to church leaders.

After the Norman Conquest, monastic communities of nuns and monks from the Anglo-Saxon era, such as the communities of Jarrow and Whitby known to Bede, were crushed in the Gregorian reform movement of Pope Gregory VII. During the High Middle Ages there was much greater institutional limitation on acceptable religious service for women, though a number of noteworthy female figures, such as Julian of Norwich, Margery Kemp, Catherine of Siena, Catherine of Genoa and Bridget of Sweden, made significant impact on popular piety. Certain 'heresies' such as the Albigensians or Cathars of thirteenth-century Europe, or the Lollards of fifteenth-century England, were persecuted in part because they challenged the norms by allowing female leadership. Even female lay groups such as the Beguines were regarded as ambiguous.

The sixteenth-century Reformation did not alter this reality very much save in a few marginal religious sects. Indeed little changed until nineteenth- and twentieth-century education and later contraception changed the status of women in western societies. The effects of these changes in roles and expectations have led some to regard them as western rather than global challenges able, therefore, to be marginalised in other parts of the Christian church. Others argue that such changes recover deeper and forgotten traditions implicit in Scripture, Baptism and Eucharist. The tensions surrounding the ordination of women to the priesthood and episcopate and the issues surrounding lesbian and gay sexuality reflect these debates, and are unlikely to be resolved in a universally agreed manner across world Christianity.

BOOKS, ETC.

Alison, James, *Faith Beyond Resentment: Fragments Catholic and Gay* (London: Darton, Longman and Todd, 2001)

Bradshaw, Timothy (ed.), *The Way Forward? Christian Voices on Homosexuality and the Church* (Hodder & Stoughton: London, 1997)

Daly, Mary, *Beyond God the Father* (London: The Woman's Press, 1985)

Davies, Jon, and Loughlin, Gerald (eds), *Sex These Days: Essays in Theology, Sexuality and Society* (Sheffield: Sheffield Academic Press, 1997)

Goddard, Andrew, *Homosexuality and the Church of England* (Cambridge: Grove Booklets, 2004)

Hastings, Adrian (ed.), *A World History of Christianity* (London: Cassell, 1999), pp. 131–7

Linzay, Andrew and Kirker, Richard (eds), *Gays and the Future of Anglicanism: Responses to the Windsor Report* (O Books, 2005)

Moberly, Elizabeth, *Homosexuality: A New Christian Ethic* (Cambridge: James Clarke, 1983)

Moore, Gareth, *A Question of Truth: Christianity and Homosexuality* (London: Continuum, 2003)

Parsons, Susan, *Feminism and Christian Ethics* (Cambridge: CUP, 1996)

Percy, Martyn (ed.), *Sexuality and Spirituality in Perspective* (London: Darton, Longman and Todd, 1997)

Stuart, Elizabeth, *Gay and Lesbian Theologies: Repetitions with Critical Difference* (Aldershot: Ashgate, 2004)

Vasey, Michael, *Strangers and Friends: A New Exploration of Homosexuality and the Bible* (London: Hodder & Stoughton, 1995)

Christianity and Industry

GORDON MORTON

Since 1944 the church has had an 'official' place in industry. The Bishop of Sheffield, Dr Leslie Hunter, appointed Ted Wickham as Industrial Chaplain to the Diocese of Sheffield. The consequence was that Industrial Mission raised many difficult and unanswered questions. It questioned the weakness of the church in industrialised areas and the apparent absence of the working class from church. The work Wickham began continues to this day in the form of Industrial Mission in South Yorkshire (IMSY). It is now ecumenical and provides a strong and valuable presence within industry today. The traditional venues for the chaplains may have changed with the demise of much manufacturing industry, yet the chaplains are still present in a wide variety of workplaces. These range from the police, fire and rescue services through to department stores and football clubs.

Wickham believed that Industrial Mission was essentially a movement in which lay and ordained are fellow workers and IMSY's chaplains demonstrate that this is as true today as it was in 1944. The chaplains provide both a prophetic and pastoral voice in the commercial world. Those whom they serve value them and they provide an important bridge to the unchurched in an increasingly secular post-modern world.

BOOKS, ETC.

Bagshaw, Paul, *The Church Beyond the Church* (Sheffield: Sheffield Design and Print, 1994)
Rogerson, John (ed.), *Industrial Mission in a Changing World* (Sheffield: Sheffield Academic Press, 1996)
Sprunger, Ben, Suter, Carol and Kroeker, Wally, *Faith Dilemmas for Marketplace Christians* (Scottdale: Pennsylvania, 1997)
Wickham, Edward R., *Church and People in an Industrial City* (London: Lutterworth, 1957)

Christianity and Race
CARMEN FRANKLIN

Have you ever thought of the many things you can change about yourself and the few things you cannot? You can change almost anything: your name, hair style and colour, your job, your habits; but you cannot change where you were born, your birth parents, your genetic make-up or the colour of your skin. Skin colour and ethnicity are regarded as the determining factors of race, today. even though Christians believe that God created only one race, the human race, all of equal worth in his sight. This division has resulted in the growth of prejudice and racism as taught behaviour. Let me illustrate:

> One bright summer's day in 1961, in Croydon, a young couple noticed a small child, walking a few paces ahead of his mother, coming towards them. As they drew closer, the child shouted, 'Mummy, mummy, look a black man and a black woman.' The mother immediately darted forward, grabbed her child, pressed his face into her skirt and stood quite still, averting her gaze as the couple passed them. Although the child had shown nothing but innocence in his outburst, the mother's response would have taught him that there is something to fear in black people. Could it be that she had ingested horror stories about black people from her elders? What a difference it would have made had she simply said, 'Yes,' and smiled at the couple.

Reflecting on the Institute of Race Relations statistics (2000/1) that black people were eight times more likely to be stopped and searched, and four times more likely to be arrested than other people, I am convinced that prejudice is playing a major part in our society. It is almost impossible to look at the state of the world and not acknowledge a fundamental cause of the violence and turmoil as prejudice and racism. Christians are called to love one another and to 'love your neighbour as yourself' (Matthew 22:39), and not to hate. This is a simple yet difficult commandment to keep – simple because it requires open hearts, and difficult because there is so much to discourage it – it is so easy to go along with the majority.

An example of how to live is found in the Antioch church (Acts 9—13), a multicultural, multi-ethnic gathering of people from a variety of backgrounds: men from Cyprus, Barnabas, Lucius from Cyrene, Manaen (brought up by Herod the tetrarch), Simeon called Niger and Saul called Paul. It was at Antioch that we were first called Christians. In Christianity there is no place for prejudice and racism. They result in unjust treatment against individuals and groups and this is sin against God. Racist behaviour is so easily learnt by the very young and nurtured by negative responses or inaction from adults, that finally it becomes a norm of society.

In 1993, the murder of 17-year-old Stephen Lawrence because he was black made headlines in the British press. The inquiry which followed brought about changes in the law but others have since met a similar fate. There is increasing movement of people across the world and injustice continues to flourish, but where is the Christian church taking a stand? Jesus Christ, a black Jew, innocent of all crime, was crucified and died for our sins over 2,000 years ago. He died that all might live. Is Christ divided? If not, then is it not time to set divisions of race aside?

BOOKS, ETC.
Beckford, Robert, *Jesus is Dread: Black Theology and Black Culture in Britain* (London: Darton, Longman and Todd, 1998)
—*Dread and Pentecostal* (London: SPCK, 2000)
—*God and the Gangs* (London: Darton, Longman and Todd, 2004)
Catholic Association for Racial Justice (CARJ), *Out of the Shadows: an audio-visual history of the Black Presence in Britain 1500–1950* (1987)
— *Unequal Access: the Housing Experience of Black People* (London: Catholic Housing Aid Society, 1993)
Cone, James, *A Black Theology of Liberation* (New York: Orbis Books, 1968)
—*My Soul Looks Back* (New York: Orbis Books, 1995)
—*God of the Oppressed* (New York: Orbis Books 2000)
Fryer, Peter, *Staying Power: the History of Black People in Britain* (London: Pluto Press, 1984)
Statistics on Race and the Criminal Justice System 2003 (London: Home Office, 2004)
Lewis, C. S., *Mere Christianity* (London: HarperCollins, 1997)
Smith, Gordon T., *Discerning God's Will in Times of Choice* (Leicester: IVP, 1997)

Christianity, Urban Life and the Mission Journey
IAN McCOLLOUGH

Oscar Romero said, 'When I feed the poor, they call me a saint; when I ask why they are poor, they call me a communist.' In the minds of many, it is in the urban areas where they expect to find a concentration of those who are not wise by human standards, not influential, not of noble birth, foolish, weak and of lowly position. They are not among the power brokers, yet Paul reminds us that God chose such as these (1 Corinthians 1:26–29).

Mission and ministry are about our response to our love of God, and reveal how we love others as ourselves, as an indication of how we fulfil the two great commandments given by Jesus (Matthew 23:34–40). The journey for the Christian is one of building relationships with God and our neighbour and allowing ourselves to be transformed through those relationships.

One of the first steps is to listen to the stories and concerns of others and, in our response, not being afraid to reveal something of ourselves to encourage the building of trust. Areas of disagreement, even dissension, can be healthy and reveal a concern and sense of commitment, whereas passivity can conceal and encourage a retreat from life.

If our mission context is an urban one, issues cannot be avoided as they press in on us, demanding a response. The Church and individuals have often listened and acted with others to meet needs with vision, courage and dedication. It is too easy to be paralysed by sheer demand, whether it is in the United Kingdom or abroad. To understand something of our part in God's preferred mission task for us, it is essential that each of us recognise that we cannot meet every need. It is better to do a small piece of work and do it well than to attempt too much and let others, and ourselves, down.

Whatever our context there will still be needs. We need to hear God's voice in discerning those local needs that, with the love and grace of God and the strength of the Holy Spirit, we, with others, might begin to meet. Wherever we live, we must not be distracted from looking for the needs in our local situation, even if they may be less evident. An aid to our thinking about our mission might be to seek out any similarities to known urban needs within our situation, whether suburban or rural. It is important to recognise that in all areas, there are people who know themselves to be in similar situations to those seen as the urban poor and feel even more isolated. Some may be living with a sense of shame or inadequacy, but many with a quiet dignity.

Jesus and Paul set their mission agenda in the context of their situations. Jesus told stories of life situations to raise the listeners' awareness of life around them, challenging the individuals and institutions of his day to relate to the reality of God. Paul told his audience in Athens what he had seen in their city and what that told him about them. He used their situation as a starting point for his dialogue with them (Acts 17:22–34).

Just as Jesus' stories focused on the value to God of the outcast and the weak, and the inability of religious institutions to engage with them as they were, so the Church, urban, rural and suburban has much to learn from those considered to be outside it, and from the possible reaction of any institutions. There are times when the Church has heard and acted on the stories it has been told, and combined its teaching and mission in practical action.

God is both resistant to our authority and impervious to religion that does not relate to those who are excluded. The challenge to us is: 'Will we continue to speak to the converted and stifle ourselves, or will we allow ourselves to grow through being challenged by new people, daring to find that God is both known and unknowable and that we can live with the paradox?' Institutions need help to become responsive: for many, their administrative machinery services their shareholders, so constraining the ability of their employees to respond to the needs of even their clients, let alone those of the wider communities where they are situated.

Sociology students sent by their professor to assess the potential future of two hundred of the poorest students in down-town Baltimore reported that they had no future because of their poverty disadvantage. Twenty-five years on, most of the two hundred still lived locally and held very good jobs. When their teacher was questioned on how she had achieved this success, she replied: 'It's simple. I just loved those children.'

To return to Oscar Romero:

A church that doesn't provoke any crisis, a Gospel that doesn't unsettle,
a word of God that doesn't get under anyone's skin,
a word of God that doesn't touch the real sin of the society around it,
what Gospel is that?
Very nice, pious considerations that don't bother anyone;
that's the way many would like preaching to be.
Yet does such a Gospel light the world we live in?
The Gospel of Christ is courageous;
it is the 'good news' of him who came to transform
and take away the world's sin.

BOOKS, ETC.

Borg, Marcus, *The Heart of Christianity* (San Francisco: HarperCollins, 2003)
Elliott, Michael C., *Freedom, Justice and Christian Counter Culture* (London: SCM, 1990)
Fung, Raymond, *The Isaiah Vision* (London: SCM, 1992)
Green, Laurie, *Urban Ministry and the Kingdom of God* (London: SPCK, 2003)
Harper, Nile, *Urban Churches: Vital Signs* (Grand Rapids MI: Eerdmans, 1999)
Nolan, Albert, *Jesus Before Christianity* (London: Darton, Longman and Todd, 1976)
Rhodes, David, *Faith in Dark Places* (London: Triangle, 1996)
Sedgwick, Peter (ed.), *God in the City* (London: Mowbray, 1995)
Wallis, Jim, *The Soul of Politics* (London: Fount, 1995)

SENDING FORTH

MISSION AND THE HOLY SPIRIT

Introduction (15mins)

Welcome and prayer.

Last Session's Challenge

Share your reflections upon the Eucharist and your life from the last session.

Aims of This Session

To reflect on the way God equips us for mission.

Liturgy

Almighty God,
we thank you for feeding us
with the body and blood of your Son Jesus Christ.
Through him we offer you our souls and bodies
to be a living sacrifice.
Send us out
in the power of the Spirit
to live and work
to your praise and glory.
Amen.

Reflection (20mins)

- What does becoming a 'living sacrifice' mean to you?
- In what ways do you detect the power of the Spirit in your service of God?
- What would you say is the particular mission of your church and what is your part in it?
- How do you connect this mission with your mission as a 'living sacrifice'?

Bible Bit (20mins)

Acts 2:1–13

(In this story St Luke describes the giving of the Holy Spirit at Pentecost which resources the early Church for sharing in the mission of God.)

• How does this passage enrich your understanding of the mission of the Church and of your experience as a living sacrifice?
• Discuss your understanding of the symbols of wind, fire and language in this passage and how they relate to your experience of God in mission.
• In what ways does your present experience of church illustrate or conflict with this passage?
• What are the implications of this passage for our belonging to the world-wide Church?

Share Spot (15mins)

Talk about the Share Spot resources for this session, which look at the themes of Holy Spirit and mission.

• How does the Holy Spirit empower the Church for mission?
• Which bit of missionary history most surprised you and why?
• What does church planting mean to you now?

Ponder Point (5mins)

What has this session clarified about your discipleship?

Prayer (5mins)

Challenge

• Find time this week to record what you have learned from this session.
• List a number of ways which would help your church to develop its mission in your area. As the fire of mission burns, what might be burned up or lost in your present church's activities?

Share Spot Resources

The Holy Spirit and Mission
SUE HOPE

'Mission means the proclamation and manifestation of Jesus' all-embracing reign – which is not yet recognised or acknowledged by all but is nevertheless already a reality.' So writes David Bosch, the missiologist (someone whose job it is to think about mission). Mission means 'making the future present' – telling forth in word and deed the power of the risen Jesus, calling men and women and children to follow him, proclaiming his power in acts of mercy, healing and forgiveness. And to do this we need the Holy Spirit: mission and the Holy Spirit belong together. That's because mission begins in the heart of God: he is a missionary God, sending his Son, sending the Spirit, sending us.

Luke and Acts are the key books when thinking about mission. Written by the same author, they form a complete whole – look in the gospel at the way Jesus interacts with people, both in word and in deed, clearly seeing himself as 'anointed by the Spirit' (Luke 4:18), and teaching his disciples that they too need the Spirit in order to minister to others (Luke 11:5–13). Before he goes back to the Father, he promises that the power of the Holy Spirit will be given to them to be his witnesses 'in Jerusalem, and in Judea and Samaria, and to the ends of the earth' (Acts 1:8), and, as we have already seen, the Spirit is poured out on the day of Pentecost (Acts 2:1–13). The rest of the book of Acts is a missionary story of how those first followers of Jesus were impelled by the Spirit out into the world. It's not so much the account of the internal organisation of the church (that's more what the epistles are about) – it's primarily a missionary book. So it's a vital book to study and reflect on as we begin to move out from our churches into missionary activity. Here are some starters!

1. The promise of the Spirit is connected with world-wide witness (Acts 1:8) – and as soon as the Spirit comes the disciples begin to speak with other tongues (2:4) and to preach (2:5–13). The Spirit and the preaching of the gospel are connected. The Spirit gives great boldness in speaking of Jesus, even when conditions are hostile (Acts 4:8ff and 31).
2. Luke tells us that Stephen was a man 'full of the Holy Spirit' (6:5) and that he combined a ministry of 'waiting on tables' (6:2), powerful signs and wonders (6:8) and fearless proclamation (7), 'full of God's grace and power' (6:8).
3. Guidance in mission to individuals was clearly under the direction of the Holy Spirit. Look, for example, at Philip and the way he was led through an unpromising wilderness to meet the Ethiopian eunuch (Acts 8:26f) and how willing he was to baptise him without much preparation (8:36)! Peter was prepared through a dream for his encounter with Cornelius (Acts 10:9–17) and through a direct word from the Spirit (10:19), and the Holy Spirit was clearly active as he told Cornelius about Jesus (10:44). There is a real sense of dependence, of partnership, of openness between the missionaries and the Spirit.
4. Guidance about the mission strategy was also by the Holy Spirit. It was the Spirit who told the church at Antioch, during worship, to 'set aside Barnabas and Saul for the work to which I have called them' (13:2). The Spirit actually

stopped them from going to one place in mission (Acts 16:6) and gave Paul a vision in the night to guide them to Macedonia (16:9). That led directly to the conversion of Lydia (16:13f). And the Spirit warned Paul of danger through the disciples at Troas (21:4).

There's lots more! Enjoy reading Acts again and reflect on these questions as you do:

* How can I/we be more open each day to the Holy Spirit leading in mission?
* Is the Holy Spirit speaking to me/us about a new 'missionary journey' to be made in the parish/at work at present?
* How can I be bold without being insensitive in sharing my faith with others?

BOOKS, ETC.

Avis, Paul, *A Ministry Shaped by Mission* (Edinburgh: T. & T. Clark, 2005)

Cray, Graham *et al.*, *Mission-shaped Church* (London: Church House Publishing, 2004)

Donovan, Vincent, *Christianity Rediscovered* (London: SCM, 1985)

Green, Michael, *I Believe in the Holy Spirit* (London: Hodder and Stoughton, 1975)

Hauerwas, Stanley, *A Better Hope: Resources for a Church Confronting Capitalism, Democracy and Postmodernity* (Michigan: Brazos Press, 2000)

Hope, Susan, *Mission-shaped Spirituality: the Transforming Power of Mission* (London: Church House Publishing, 2006)

Jackson, Bob, *Hope for the Church: Contemporary Strategies for Growth* (London: Church House Publishing, 2002)

—*Explorations: The Road to Growth: Towards a Thriving Church* (London: Church House Publishing, 2005)

Morgan, A., *The Wild Gospel* (Oxford: Monarch, 2004)

Morisy, Ann, *Beyond the Good Samaritan* (London: Mowbray, 1997)

—*Journeying Out: A New Approach to Christian Mission* (London: Morehouse, 2004)

Moynagh, Michael, *Changing World, Changing Church: New Forms of Church out-of-the-pew Thinking Initiatives that Work* (London: Monarch Books, 1998)

Warren, Robert, *Being Human, Being Church: Spirituality and Mission in the Local Church* (London: Marshall Pickering, 1995)

Wimber, John and Springer, Kevin, *Power Evangelism* (London: Hodder and Stoughton, 1985)

And any biography of missionary journeys – see for example the life of St Francis of Assisi, Hudson Taylor, Amy Carmichael ...

The History of Christian Mission
GABRIELLE DE VREESE

'Go, make disciples of all nations,' are the words of Jesus as recorded in Matthew's Gospel, forming the foundation on which many missionary organisations base their work, particularly in more recent centuries. This is known as the Great Commission, but it was Luke who wrote the first history of the Christian mission, beginning with 'all that Jesus began to do and teach' (Acts 1:1) in his Gospel. He went on to describe some of the achievements of the early Apostles, such as Peter and John, and the extensive, zealous missionary work of Paul.

From out of the early Christian Church come tumbling a host of successors to the Apostles, spreading the gospel message of salvation to the peoples in the surrounding areas. Eusebius (d. *c.*339) describes some of them in his *Ecclesiastical History*, naming 'shepherds', i.e. the church leaders, and 'evangelists', meaning the travelling missionaries. Throughout the centuries the Christian Church has continued to proclaim Christ as Saviour, as much by quiet witness of works as by more overt missionary activity.

By the fourth century AD the Church was also thriving in Britain, probably brought by the Romans, but developing its own distinctive Celtic style. This is highlighted by figures such as Patrick (d. 461), missionary to the Irish, and Columba (d. 597), who established a monastery in western Scotland as a base to convert fellow Scots and the Picts. Both were visionaries with notable success, who set out to influence first the local kings and chieftains as a means to winning over their tribes and clans. They were followed by other great men and women in the early British church, such as Aidan (d. 651) and Hilda (d. 680), who forwarded the work in northeastern England.

At the initiative of Pope Gregory I, head of the church in Rome, missionary activity was spread to southern England by the arrival in 597 of that reluctant missionary, Augustine. He converted the royal household, thereby establishing the faith among the Anglo-Saxons. Missionaries from the British church engaged in missions to Europe.

The following centuries tell us little of the expansion of the Christian Church. For instance, we know that Boniface took the gospel to Germany, founding an abbey at Fulda in 744, and this became a centre for missionary work, including among the Scandinavian and Slav countries. But it was a dark time in history, with Europe and the Middle East struggling against disasters such as the various invasions of the barbarians.

The dawn of the second millennium was darkened by the activity of the Crusades. The rise of Islam coupled profound religious faith with zeal for lands, and the Muslim conquests caused a major setback for the Christian world. For two hundred years, in the name of delivering the holy places from the hands of unbelievers, warring expeditions were led against the Muslims. Basically, they failed in their aims. Rather than expanding Christian Europe, they permanently injured the relationship between east and west, a legacy which continues today. But other Christian missions continued, even as far as East Asia. Much of the work was from England, for example, as a result of the Viking conquests bringing closer contact with the English, and thereby their church.

The Reformation was precisely that – a long period of Church reform throughout the west, not so much concerned with pagan souls being saved, as with Christians understanding their salvation. It marked the divide between Protestant austerity and Catholic flamboyance, between a centring on the biblical word of God and the sacraments. By the sixteenth century, the shaken-up Roman Catholic Church began its missions to the New World. The great religious orders, most notably the Jesuits, played a leading part in the spiritual conquest both there and in the Orient. Since they enjoyed royal protection, financial and political help was generous.

As time went on, generally speaking, the established Protestant church objected to emotional responses to the receiving of the love of God. It had also slid into being politically stifled, so it was no wonder that it was threatened by a new age of renewal in the eighteenth century. In Britain this movement was called the Evangelical or Methodist Revival. In North America, where it began, it was called the Great Awakening. Preachers such as Jonathan Edwards, John and Charles Wesley and George Whitefield drew great crowds, often hundreds, meeting in fields surrounding the towns.

The industrial age heralded a series of Christian societies, such as the Salvation Army, which were founded to take social aid as well as spiritual succour to an impoverished working class. Overseas missionary societies were also formed, to take the gospel to the 'heathen' in the British colonies throughout the world, particularly India, Africa and China. However, well-meaning missionaries tended to impose western values, culture and church practices on their converts, and this was not properly addressed until the latter part of the twentieth century. Other societies, such as the Bible Society, undertook translating the Bible into common languages both at home and abroad. Many of these societies continue to exist today, as the needs remain, though finding new funding can be difficult.

By the end of the second millennium, Christian belief had more competition than ever, with the firm establishment of other great world religions and the inexorable march of advances in science, medicine and world communication. A Christian world was no longer a given, though mass crusades with preachers such as the well-respected Billy Graham did their best to stem the flow away from Christian truth to pagan practice and atheistic indifference.

However, what has marked Christian mission as being distinctive from all the rest is that, despite persecution, abuse of power, divisions and dissent, the message of God's kingdom of love has continued to flourish. And through the power of the Holy Spirit, there will always be believers called to proclaim God's message of truth and hope by witness and by word.

BOOKS, ETC.

Bowen, Roger, *So I Send You – A Study Guide to Mission* (London: SPCK, 1998)
Cromby, J., *How to Read Church History*, vol. 1 (London: SCM, 1985); vol. 2 (London: SCM, 1989)

Dowley, Tim and Alexander, Pat, *The History of Christianity* (London: Lion, 1977)
Neill, Stephen, *A History of Christian Missions* (London: Penguin, 1990)

Church Planting Today
GEORGE LINGS

Only fifteen years ago some church planters were literally met with the objection that Augustine of Canterbury had completed this task in 597 AD. Such ecclesiastical complacency and contemporary missionary ignorance is increasingly incredible.

WHAT IS CHURCH PLANTING?
Church planting is part of the Church being apostolic – that is being sent to bring the Christian faith to groups of people who do not know it, in order to create fresh communities that express the Kingdom of God. This theological conviction underlies contemporary church planting. In one way it is what the Church has always done. From a world-wide perspective it is not new, not even in the Anglican context, where a parochial system can be misused to delude us into thinking everybody is provided for. The gap between being legally in a parish and being spiritually positively influenced by the local church is vast. Many plants have been created to attempt to narrow the chasm.

WHO DOES IT?
Church planting is practised by those, in virtually all denominations, who recognise the emergence of a post-Christian society. The Church of England alone has sent out teams which created some four hundred new churches, and thereby in effect created a new membership equivalent to a fair-sized diocese. As reported in Springboard's *There Are Answers* (p. 7) and Bob Jackson's *Hope for the Church*, church planting has brought the most vigorous growth of congregations seen in this country. Numbers are not everything, but these churches are a base for the desirable full engagement in all the dimensions of mission, together with growth in depth and quality. Church plants have been one of the good news stories in the Church, showing that she can still multiply.

Church planting is increasingly diverse. Past stereotypes portrayed it as a theologically indecent charismatic invasion of parochial boundaries, done by large groups from large churches, merely exporting their existing preferences. The reality is that it is practised by all traditions in the Church of England, the average team size is 20, and 99 per cent of church plants happen with full diocesan and local permission. Helpfully, there is increasing awareness that the formation of expressions of church which genuinely fit the culture served is far more important than copying what other Christians like. Often called 'Fresh Expressions', the present range includes alternative worship groups, base ecclesial communities, café churches, cell churches, community development based churches, midweek and multiple diverse congregations, network churches, new monastic communities, school-based churches, seeker churches, so-called traditional church plants and youth congregations.[1] They serve different groups in a diversifying society. They are responses to society being reconfigured in networks as well as neighbourhoods. As such, they push the boundaries of what is acceptable Anglican diversity, but the essence of their Anglican identity is the desire to be localised and incarnational, as well as relational and Episcopal. The Archbishop of Canterbury, Rowan Williams, has publicly called for the creation of 'mixed economy' thinking for existing and emerging churches to embrace one another. The Church of England's *Mission-Shaped Church* Report has opened up fresh discussion and action in this area and the Archbishops' Fresh Expressions initiative is seeking to facilitate these explorations.

The leading provider of courses for Anglicans who want to understand church plants and their dynamics, is at the Church Army's Training College in Sheffield. Baptists would look to Spurgeon's College in London. But both places have an ecumenical range of students.

BOOKS, ETC.

Cray, Graham *et al.*, *Mission-shaped Church* (London: Church House Publishing, 2004)

Hopkins, Bob, *Cell Church Stories as Signs of Mission* (Nottingham: Grove Evangelism No. 51)

Hopkins, Bob *et al.*, *Planting New Churches* (Eagle, 1991)

Harris, Patrick *et al.*, *Breaking new Ground: House of Bishops Report* (London: Church House Publishing, 1994)

Jackson, Bob, *Hope for the Church: Contemporary Strategies for Growth* (London: Church House Publishing, 2002)

Moynagh, Michael, *Emergingchurch.intro* (Oxford: Monarch, 2004)

Murray, Stuart, *Church Planting – Laying Foundations* (Carlisle: Paternoster, 1998)

The widest range of case studies of Fresh Expressions church plants is found at the website of the Church Army's Research Unit at the Sheffield Centre, www.encountersontheedge .org.uk . See also the Fresh Expressions website: www.freshexpressions.org.uk

---

[1] See Graham Cray *et al.*, *Mission-shaped Church* (London: Church House Publishing, 2004), chapter 4, pp. 43ff for examples and descriptions of all these.

MISSION AND THE GOOD NEWS

Introduction (15mins)

Welcome and prayer.

Last Session's Challenge
Share your list of mission possibilities made during the past week.

Aim of This Session
To explore evangelism, or 'sharing the Gospel', as the heart of mission.

Liturgy

The peace of God which passes all understanding, keep your hearts and minds in the knowledge and love of God, and of his Son Jesus Christ our Lord: and the blessing of God almighty, the Father, the Son and the Holy Spirit, be among you and remain with you always. Amen.

Reflection (20mins)

- What do you understand by the peace and blessing of God the Holy Trinity?
- How do you and your church embody and share the peace and blessing of God bestowed upon you in worship?
- How could this be described as good news (Gospel) for your neighbourhood and the wider world?
- How do you think most people in your church's neighbourhood rate you as a good-news community and what would improve this rating?

Bible Bit (20mins)

Acts 2:14–42
(This is the second half of Luke's Pentecost passage and connects the gift of the Spirit with the establishment of the church in mission.)

- Who is this sermon aimed at, and what does this suggest about how we share the Gospel in our context?
- What gives credibility to Peter's sermon?
- How does Peter's sharing of the Gospel relate to or challenge the way you embody and share the Gospel as a church and as an individual?
- For whom is this Gospel and how is it to be shared?

Share Spot (15mins)

Talk about the Share Spot resources for this session, which reflect on evangelism (sharing the good news).

- What does evangelism mean to you?
- What are the challenges facing Christians seeking to share the Gospel today?
- Why might cults prove attractive to spiritual seekers?
- What encouragements and challenges does the world church give to Christians living in the United Kingdom?

Ponder Point (5mins)

What has this session clarified about your discipleship?

Prayer (5mins)

Challenge

- Find time this week to record what you have learned from this session.
- Looking at your church, your own life and your neighbourhood, write down in one sentence what you think is the heart of the Gospel or Good News for your church, yourself and your neighbourhood.

Share Spot Resources

Evangelism Today
GARY WILTON

Evangelism – the very mention of the word often provokes an instant reaction. Often people's first thought is 'Billy Graham', the second, 'door knocking' and the third, 'it's not for me!'

The Decade of Evangelism was an important time, not least because it put evangelism on the agenda. It has also made us think again about how we understand this vital ministry. We have rediscovered that evangelism belongs to the ministry of the whole church: catholic, central, evangelical, liberal or conservative, high and low. It's not a job simply for evangelists or clergy or readers, but is the concern of every Christian.

The Decade made us question our use of resources. How much do we spend on maintenance? How much do we spend on mission and evangelism? How many person hours do we spend on caring for our buildings? How many hours do we commit to reaching out to the people around us? We need to keep asking these questions.

One of the biggest lessons of recent years has been the fresh recognition that evangelism is often a process or a journey. Whilst many people have a 'conversion' experience, the majority come to faith over a much longer period. We have begun to see evangelism as a process, which may include a great variety of small steps forward as well as some back. Thinking again, we can often see that a conversion experience is actually a very important moment within a much longer process of God drawing us to himself.

A whole number of evangelistic and nurture courses have been developed to assist individuals on their journey. The Alpha and Emmaus courses in particular have been very widely used across churches of every tradition. They both seek to support individuals through the process of coming to faith, answering their questions along the way and introducing them to the life of the Church. Emmaus, based on Luke 24, especially uses the language of journey throughout the course.

Ann Morisy, in her book *Beyond the Good Samaritan*, has also influenced much of today's thinking about evangelism. She is convinced that church community projects developed with secular partners are a good thing. She is also clear that community projects can be an important part of evangelistic ministry to those being helped. She points out that as Christians we have very important things to say to our project partners, and argues that frequently we hide our lights under bushels. We just do not share what we did on Sunday or what we learnt during the Lent course, or discuss with them why we want to be involved. Sometimes we exclude our project partners from the Good News that has made a such difference to us. She challenges us to put this right.

To date much of our evangelism has focused on people coming to church to be evangelised. The massive cultural changes in the last quarter of the twentieth century mean that the future needs to be more about going out to share faith rather than inviting people to come in. The cultural gap between the church as we know it and wider society has become a gulf. For most people the church is not even on their social or spiritual radar. Non-Christians will simply not come to church to be evangelised. Mark Greene in particular has important things to say about being a Christian at work today. So much of our teaching and preaching is about being church – he challenges us to think about being Christians in the world. Being a Christian at work is not only personally challenging but full of potential opportunities to share and demonstrate the Good News. If you have not read *Thank God its Monday*, it's a must!

At the same time the recent discussions about the *Mission-Shaped Church* Report have also helped us to realise that much of our evangelism in the future will involve fresh expressions of church. Relationships and process will continue to be important, but church as we know it will need to evolve to include new times, new places and new ways of being church to capture the imaginations of the new generations of unchurched people!

BOOKS, ETC.

Cray, Graham *et al.*, *Mission-shaped Church* (London: Church House Publishing, 2004)
Booker, Mike and Ireland, Mark, *Evangelism – Which Way Now?* (London: Church House Publishing, 2003)
Cottrell, Stephen, *Catholic Evangelism* (London: Darton, Longman and Todd, 1998)
Greene, Mark, *Thank God's It's Monday* (London: Scripture Union, 1998)
Jamieson, Alan, *A Churchless Faith* (London: SPCK 2002)
Morisy, Ann, *Beyond the Good Samaritan* (London: Mowbray,1997)
—*Journeying Out: A New Approach to Christian Mission* (London: Morehouse, 2004)
Tomlin, Graham, *The Provocative Church* (London: SPCK, 2002)

Alpha (Holy Trinity Brompton, London)
Emmaus (The Bible Society)

The Gospel in Society

IAN MAHER

If William Shakespeare were suddenly to appear in England today, he would be semi-literate. Language has changed and the world is a very different place. To survive he would need to learn about society as it is today. He would need a new framework, a new worldview, in order to make sense of his experience.

In some respects, the pace of change in society over the last few decades, accelerated phenomenally by the information technology revolution, poses to all of us a similar challenge if the Gospel is to speak relevantly into the needs of today. While the heart of the Gospel message is timeless, its effective communication will be inextricably bound up with our insights and understanding of contemporary society. Some key features of Western society at the beginning of the twenty-first century are individualism, materialism, and the cultural shift from modernity to post-modernity.

The roots of individualism and materialism can be traced to the Enlightenment and to the Industrial Revolution. Human reason became the unchallenged point of departure for all knowing; an unshakeable belief emerged in the inevitability of progress, modernisation and development; and science achieved an almost god-like status. As people became regarded as emancipated, autonomous individuals the market economy thrived, leading to the 'triumph' of capitalism. While individualism and materialism continue to thrive in some respects, the philosophical foundations on which they are premised are creaking at the seams.

Two World Wars, the widening gulf between rich and poor and the decimation of our environment, have highlighted the flaw in the utopian dream of evolution towards paradise on earth. Even the unshakeable certainties of science have become open to question and criticism. Neither the rational human mind nor empirical evidence have been able to provide all the answers to the question of what it means for human beings to live together on this earth. The age of modernity, characterised by some of the features mentioned above, appears to be passing away. Exactly what will replace it is unclear, and this has resulted in the expression 'post-modernity'. This is a time of transition, but some features of post-modernity are beginning to emerge.

Human reason is no longer regarded by many as being able to answer the big questions of life in the way that rationalism sought to do, and the concept of objective truth is being rejected. As the limitations of scientific explanation become apparent, stories are increasingly seen as vehicles for interpreting the world and finding meaning. Far more attention is being paid to the non-rational aspects of human existence.

Post-modernity rejects any attempt to impose an overarching framework of understanding, or 'meta-narrative', upon the way the world is. In that respect the truth is not out there but is something that people make for themselves in order to make sense of the world around them. A consequence of this shift in perspective is a rejection of authority, evident in the decline of many traditional institutions. It may go some way towards explaining the decline in church attendance, despite a mushrooming interest in spirituality in modern society where there is now a veritable supermarket of choice. The proliferation of the diverse New Age Movement is a clear example of this.

This is the society with which Christians are called to engage the Gospel. It is a very different one from that which our grandparents, and maybe even our parents, knew. The challenge is to find new ways of telling and re-telling the Christian story in a society where the certainties of modernity are passing away.

BOOKS, ETC.

Atkinson, David, *God so Loved the World* (Lynx, 1999)

Drane, John, *The McDonaldization of the Church* (London: Darton, Longman and Todd, 2000)

—*Creativity and the Future of the Church* (London: Darton, Longman & Todd, 2003)

Gibbs, Eddie and Coffey, Ian, *Church Next: Quantum Changes in Christian Ministry* (Leicester: IVP, 2001)

Grenz, S., *A Primer on Postmodernism* (Grand Rapids MI: Eerdmans, 1996)

Moynagh, Michael, *Changing World, Changing Church: New Forms of Church out-of-the-pew Thinking Initiatives that Work* (London: Monarch Books, 1998)

Sire, J. W., *The Universe Next Door*, 3rd edn (Leicester: Inter-Varsity Press, 1997)

The Church and Cults
PEDR BECKLEY

In the world of the social sciences cults, sects, and alternative religions have technical definitions, and in the popular mind the word 'cult' has a very negative feel to it. In order to create a fairly neutral title the term 'New Religious Movement' (NRM) was coined. This is used for groups that have become visible in their present form since the Second World War, and are clearly religious since they offer answers to some of the ultimate questions of life, such as 'Is there a God?', 'What is the meaning of life?' and 'What happens to us when we die?' This loose definition includes 'atheistic' religions such as various forms of Buddhism and the Human Potential Movement, as well as all sorts of variant forms of Hinduism, Christianity, the Occult and so on.

New religions have, of course, appeared throughout the course of history and today is no different except for the sheer number and diversity of these new movements. This diversity is shown in the leadership; some old, some young, some male, some female, some poor, some rich, and from all over the world. Some groups live in communes, some very individualistically. Some may indulge in sexual orgies while others lead ascetic lives. Some groups are large with thousands of members, while others can count on only 20–30 members.

If groups are so diverse, so also are the beliefs and the demands made on their memberships. Some groups are harmful while others are not and the sorts of groups that make the news are often those who are very strange and sometimes quite dangerous. In Britain alone, there are probably over 1,000 active NRMs exhibiting all the diversity mentioned above.

The Church reacts to these movements in a variety of ways. Sometimes there is the need to speak out because of them. Sometimes there is a need for pastoral care of those affected by people joining a group. Sometimes there is a need for education or advice. The Church of England, along with other denominations, the Home Office and others have set up an organisation called INFORM that works to educate, advise, care for and generally help people caught up in NRMs. In each Anglican Diocese there is a representative who is available to offer advice, counselling, and so on to those who need it. The challenge of NRMs to the Church is considerable since they indicate that many people are looking elsewhere for their spiritual needs to be met. This raises all sorts of questions that need to be looked at carefully in relation to our worship, fellowship and mission.

BOOKS, ETC.
Barker, Eileen, *New Religious Movements: A Practical Introduction* (HMSO)
Barrett, David V., *The New Believers: Sects, 'Cults' and Alternative Religions* (London: Cassell Illustrated, 2003)
Beckley, Pedr, *Mission in a Conspiracy Culture* (Cambridge: Grove Booklets, 2002)

Mission and the Overseas Church
PATRICK COGHLAN

'In vast areas of the world, the church of Jesus Christ is growing rapidly, in others it is declining gradually, and in a few others it is declining catastrophically' (David Barrett).

* There are 65 new congregations a day around the world.
* In Africa there are 16,400 new Christians a day.
* There is a loss of 7,600 Christians a day in Europe and North America.
* The world-wide Anglican church is growing at 3,000 new Christians a day.
* This is a growth of 4,000 new Christians a day in Africa and Asia and a loss of 1,000 a day in Europe and North America.
* The average Anglican is aged 20–30, is brown-skinned and lives in the Third World.
* Today 60 per cent of Anglican Dioceses are in Africa, Asia and Latin America.
* Speaking fifty years ago, Archbishop William Temple said, 'the great new fact of our era ... a Christian fellowship which now extends into almost every nation.'

All thought of a post-Christian world is 'glib ... naive and hasty' (K. S. Latourette). However, there are still many places in the world with few Christians, especially in what is called the 10–40 box (10–40° north of the equator). Indeed, in Europe there are also places with few practising Christians. Rotherham in South Yorkshire has a population of 250,000 but only 7,500 people attend church. In 1998 only 3.45 per cent of the population attended church, the lowest in the United Kingdom. Even this low percentage is declining rapidly.

In his enthronement sermon, Archbishop David Gitari (Church of the Province of Kenya) said:

> ... those in authority are quite happy when the church participates in education, health, agriculture, famine relief and other humanitarian activities. But the moment we ask what is the root cause of poverty, ignorance, disease and death some politicians will tell us to keep away from politics and confine ourselves to purely spiritual matters. Our biblical understanding is that a human being is a psychosomatic unit. He is composed of spirit and body and the two cannot be separated. The Church has the duty and the mandate to address itself to matters spiritual, as well as matters physical.

This holistic approach has contributed to the rapid growth of the Anglican church in Kenya. If we are to capture something of the breadth of Jesus' vision for mission we need to look carefully at a number of passages from the Bible, each with their different emphases.

1. Jesus announced his ministry at Nazareth: Luke 4:16–21.
   How in practice did Jesus carry out this programme of ministry?
2. Jesus then involved others in his ministry: Luke 10:1–12.
   How do you think the 72 felt about this new experience?
   In the Church of the Province of Kenya, words and actions fit together. Is this true of your church? If not, is there anything you could do so that people outside the church could experience God's love in word and action?
3. After his resurrection, Jesus spoke to the disciples: Matthew 28:16–20.
   Who did Jesus send out on his mission and to whom?
   Why do you think the church in other parts of the world is more confident in doing this?
3. In John's gospel Jesus still speaks of sending: John 20:19–23.
   What is the connection between the promise of the Holy Spirit and the message of forgiveness?

Find out about one of the links your church has with the world church. This may be a link through a mission agency or through diocesan links.

* Where is the link?
* Does your church support an individual or a project?
* How does your experience of this link encourage your faith?
* What is the difference in the way they live out their Christian faith?

In England we are used to religious freedom. However, in many parts of the world the church is being persecuted. For example in 1979 the Shah of Iran was overthrown by Ayatollah Khomeni and Islamic fundamentalism dominated for nearly twenty years. In 1994 Bishop Haik Hovsepian-Mehr was martyred and the General Superintendent of the Assemblies of God was murdered. Yet despite these difficulties the church in Iran has experienced unprecedented growth. In many of the capital cities of Europe there are growing and vibrant Iranian congregations ('A Challenge to the British Church from the World Church', Bryan Knell, *Church Growth Digest*, vol. 21 no. 1).

> Jesus said, 'Blessed are you when people insult you, persecute you and falsely say all kinds of evil things against you because of me. Rejoice and be glad, because great is your reward in heaven, for in the same way they persecuted the prophets who were before you.' (Matthew 5:11–12)

PARTNERSHIP IN WORLD MISSION
For many years mission was 'from the West to the rest'. However, as we have already seen this is no longer the case, although this thinking persists in many congregations. In 1978 the Church of England set up Partners in World Mission. This title reminds us that we all have something to give and something to learn about God's

mission in the world. Christians from around the world have summarised mission as:

- To proclaim the good news of the Kingdom of God.
- To teach, baptise and nurture new believers.
- To respond to human need by loving service.
- To seek to transform the unjust structures of society.
- To strive to safeguard the integrity of creation and sustain and renew the life of the earth.

BOOKS, ETC.

Davie, Grace, *Religion in Modern Europe: A Memory Mutates* (Oxford: OUP, 2000)
—*Europe: The Exceptional Case: Parameters of Faith in the Modern World* (London: Darton, Longman and Todd, 2002)
Donovan, Vincent, *Christianity Rediscovered* (London: SCM, 1982)
Gaukroger, Stephen, *Why Bother with Mission?* (Leicester: IVP, 1996)
Yohannan, K. P., *Revolution in World Mission* (GFA Books, 1986)

God's Global City: A Five Session Course on Mission in the Worldwide Church (London: Church House Publishing, 1997) (video and Bible study)
The World Christian, a short extension course from St John's, Nottingham.
Broken Image (video), 4 discussion starters on urban Third World issues

MISSION AND SERVICE

Introduction (15mins)

Welcome and prayer.

Last Session's Challenge
Share your snapshot of the Gospel.

Aim of This Session
To explore how mission and service belong together.

Liturgy

Go in peace to love and serve the Lord.
In the name of Christ. Amen.

Reflection (20mins)

* What does it mean for you peaceably to love and serve the Lord?
* Is there any difference between how you do this and how the church does this?
* What sort of peaceable living is possible in our sort of world and how do you think Christians should respond to challenges to peaceable living?
* In what way, if any, do you think Christian service differs from other forms of service?
* How could your church improve the quality of Christian service it offers to the neighbourhood and to wider society?

Bible Bit (20mins)

Acts 2:43–47
(This is the concluding section of the Pentecost story which describes the earliest expression of Christian community.)

- How does this story of a Christian community relate to your experience of church today?
- From this passage, what changes in your life and your church's life might make you a more convincing good-news community?
- What forms of service are listed in this passage?
- What consequences flowed from such service?
- Are there any reasons why you might not be an identical community to this one?

Share Spot (15mins)

Talk about the Share Spot resources for this session, which look at ways of loving and serving our neighbours.

- Why does Jesus place such store on loving our neighbours?
- How is your church a witness to your parish?
- In what ways could you develop links with your local schools?

Ponder Point (5mins)

What has this session clarified about your discipleship?

Prayer (5mins)

Conclusion

Congratulations on completing DOXA.

Where or What Next?

- Find time this week to record what you have learned from this session.
- Consider meeting once more, having listed the ten most significant things you have discovered about your faith by doing DOXA. Consider arranging for your local priest to preside at a group Eucharist, preferably with other DOXA groups from the church.
- At this session think together about where you might go in your discipleship as a result of doing this course. Take a large sheet of paper and record what you think. Then stand together and, holding the paper, ask God for courage to be faithful to his call.
- Consider reading some of the Share Spot books and other resources.

Share Spot Resources
Love of God, Love of Neighbour
JOHN WRAW

"'Love the Lord your God with all your heart and with all your soul and with all your mind." This is the first and greatest commandment. And the second is like it: "Love your neighbour as yourself."'
(Matthew 22:34ff, Mark 12:28ff, Luke 10:25ff)

Whether recorded on the lips of Jesus in Matthew and Mark, or on the lips of the questioning lawyer in Luke, these two separate statements from the Law of Moses (Deuteronomy 6:5, Leviticus 19:18) have throughout the centuries been regarded by the Christian community as a summary of the law, Christ's demands on his followers.

Traditionally the Ten Commandments have been divided into love for God and love for neighbour. However in the books of the prophets love for God is expressed not through worship and sacrifices, but by ethical living, care for the weak and the oppressed.

Following in this tradition, the two are quite deliberately brought together in the New Testament. We express our love for God through loving our neighbour. Teresa of Avila expressed it well: 'Christ has no hands on earth but yours ...' Our love of God leads us to do his will in his world – to care for the poor and oppressed, the sick and the dying, the widow and the orphan. The care we show is a measure of our love for God. He who does not love his brother or sister whom he has seen, cannot love God whom he has not seen (1 John 4:20).

However Christian tradition links the two even more firmly. It is in the face of the needy that we meet Christ himself, as he describes in the parable of the sheep and the goats – 'what you do for the least of my brethren you do for me.' It is a recurrent theme in Christian folklore and in the lives of the saints. Francis in kissing the leper is forever after convinced that he has met Christ. Mother Teresa sees Jesus in the sick and the dying she tends. The mystical and the practical come together.

Love for our neighbour is a participation in the divine love, the eternal dance of love in the Trinity that embraces the whole of creation. But it is love in the particular which is both challenging and manageable. Jesus responds to those he meets. The Samaritan cares for the man he sees at the roadside. The call to love is the loving in the need we meet, that we are confronted with in everyday living.

The call to love is also intensely practical. Raymond Fung in *The Isaiah Vision* outlines the aspirations of the vision in Isaiah 65, that children may grow up in safety and security, that the old may live out their lives in reasonable comfort, that people may have work and a degree of satisfaction in their work, that all may have a roof over their heads. These are little more than the basic needs of life. Yet if they were universally available the world would be transformed.

BOOKS, ETC.

A Place of Refuge: A Positive Approach to Asylum Seekers and Refugees in the UK (London: Church House Publishing, 2005)

Fung, Raymond, *The Isaiah Vision: Ecumenical Strategy for Congregational Evangelism* (Geneva: World Council of Churches, 1992)

Hauerwas, Stanley, and Willimon, William H., *The Truth About God: The Ten Commandments in Christian Life* (Nashville: Abingdon Press, 1999)

Morisy, Ann, *Beyond the Good Samaritan* (London: Mowbray, 1997)

Parish Evangelism
JOHN THOMSON

THE VALUE OF BEING THERE
Familiarity can breed contempt, but this does not need to be so in the case of the parish as an evangelistic context. If there is any clear theology of mission explicit in Church of England structures it is about being in the midst of ordinary life, reflective of God becoming flesh in Jesus Christ at a particular time, in a particular place and among a particular people. This is what Wesley Carr calls mission in pastoral mode. In addition, this has come to be understood as being committed in ministry, service and mission as the Church for England to the nation of England. As the Church of England, we have been around, we remain around and we continue to be available! Hence the importance of local structures committed to manageable 'turf', which give focus to evangelism and follow-up. Whilst not the only context of mission, notions of the death of the parish unit are somewhat premature! Certainly the mobile culture we inhabit has undermined the ancient value of this sense of belonging, yet whether as an ancient monument or as a place of continuity in the midst of a sea of change, as parish churches we continue to connect with a majority of the population. The significance of this presence, arguably dating back to the arrival of Christianity, should not be underestimated. Archbishop Rowan Williams' vision of a 'mixed economy church', together with the Church of England's *Mission-Shaped Church* Report, embraces the continuing parochial ministry as well as fresh expressions of church and sector ministry.

Nevertheless, the success or failure in any parish's evangelism is related to the way in which that parish nurtures and develops its relationship and involvement with its locality. Among other things, high-quality ministry at the occasional offices and a strategy to improve interpersonal and church contact with those served in this way are particularly important. Though often criticised for too lax an approach, Anglican generosity here seems to pay off as confidence and acceptance often precede deeper commitments. The welcome and feel of church services is also a factor in the integration of enquirers. To be an evangelistic parish involves being a parish worth joining! This is particularly important given the 'process model' of conversion emphasised by John Finney and others. Worship is evangelistic, even if it is not simply or solely evangelism.

PARISH EVANGELISM AS THE CHURCH OF ENGLAND

Such evangelism would not be possible if the parish as the expression of the local commitment of the Church of England was not in place. Even numerically weak parishes can be involved as we mutually support each other in people, plant and resources. Local presence enables distinctive sharing in local ways at schools, pubs, clubs, etc., which might otherwise be suspicious, recognising that parish evangelism is not about cult-type brainwashing, but simply about people they often know sharing the love of God. What is apparent, though, is that service rather than privilege has to be the basis upon which the parish, as representative of the Church of England, bears witness. Our history is too ambiguous to trade casually upon.

Nevertheless, our buildings in many cases do aid our cause and should not be seen simply as architectural albatrosses around our necks, just as the parish system, connected with the sign of the ordained ministry, still has great value. To have been around for so long and still to be here offers great opportunities for sharing the Gospel with most of this land. Parish evangelism is not the whole of evangelism. Fresh expressions of church, sector ministry, national witness, theological conversations with other wisdoms and the dispersed evangelism of ordinary Christian people are part of this wider evangelistic mission. However, the parish has a particularly fertile role as that tangible expression of the church at worship and in service which acts as a light of the Gospel in a given locality.

BOOKS, ETC.

Cray, Graham *et al.*, *Mission-shaped Church* (London: Church House Publishing, 2004)

Croft, Steven, *Transforming Christian Communities: Re-imagining the Church for the 21st Century* (London: Darton, Longman and Todd, 2002)

Dormor, Duncan, McDonald, Jack and Caddick, Jeremy (eds), *Anglicanism: The Answer to Modernity* (London: Continuum, 2003)

Finney, John, *Finding Faith Today* (Swindon: Bible Society, 1992)

Moynagh, Michael, *Changing World, Changing Church: New Forms of Church out-of-the-pew Thinking Initiatives that Work* (London: Monarch Books, 1998)

Sherwin, David, *A Prayer-Evangelism Strategy* (Cambridge: Grove Booklets, 1994)

Sherwin, David, Currin, Jim and Thomson, John, *Evangelism Across the Diocese: Two Diocesan Initiatives in Evangelism* (Cambridge: Grove Booklets, 1996)

Sykes, Stephen, *Unashamed Anglicanism* (London: Darton, Longman and Todd, 1995)

Sykes, Stephen and Booty, John (eds), *The Study of Anglicanism* (London: SCM, 1989)

Thomson, John B., *Church on Edge? Practising Christian Ministry Today* (Darton, Longman and Todd, 2004)
Warren, Robert, *Building Missionary Congregations*, Board of Mission and Unity Occasional Paper 4 (1995)
—*Being Human, Being Church* (London: Marshall Pickering, 1995)
Whale, John, *The Future of Anglicanism* (Oxford: OUP, 1988)

Mission and Education

MALCOLM ROBERTSON

This piece is offered as an encouragement to those who may wish to become involved in education, whether professionally or voluntarily, as part of their Christian service and witness.

Nationally, education has a high profile. Although there is debate regarding some of the methodology (OFSTED, league tables, curriculum prescription, etc.), there is a genuine concern shared by all to raise educational standards. Central government is warmly welcoming faith groups as partners. The Green Paper (February 2001) 'Schools – Building On Success' stated, 'We therefore wish to welcome more schools provided by the churches and other major faith groups ... where there is clear local demand from parents and the community.'

Our task as Christians is how to respond appropriately, within our own specific setting, whether as individuals, parishes or as a diocese, to the opportunities that are before us for Christian involvement in education. An initial word of warning: great harm can be done to parish–school relations and to the credibility of Church involvement in education quite unintentionally through inappropriate approaches, action or language. Leading school worship is a potential minefield but it is also a tremendous opportunity.

For convenience we will confine ourselves to involvement in statutory school education (primary and secondary). A clear distinction must be made between denominational (church) schools and non-denominational (community) schools. Both are part of the maintained education system, but there is a marked difference in what is appropriate between the two different categories.

For example, a Foundation Governor of a church school would be there to ensure the Christian foundation of the school is maintained, in addition to assisting with the governance of the school. A Christian who is a governor of a community school is there to serve the good of the school, not to promote his or her faith. However, there may be occasions when it would be right to reflect a Christian perspective, perhaps when the governing body is discussing the school's sex education policy.

In November 1998 the General Synod passed a major resolution that stated: '... that Church schools stand at the centre of the Church's mission to the nation'. One crucial outcome of the synod debate was the establishment of the Church

School Review Group, chaired by Lord Dearing. The final report from the Review Group, *The Way Ahead*, is essential reading for an understanding of Church schools at the beginning of the twenty-first century. The report highlights a number of key areas, one of which is parishes clearly articulating 'what it means to be a Christian teacher and, in appropriate cases, encourag[ing] a vocation to teach' (6.26).

There is a great need for Christians to serve as teachers in both church and community schools. As has been clearly stated: '... the Diocese has a commitment to all schools, both community and church, and wishes to see them all thrive.' Equally there are many ways in which individuals and parishes can, as Christians, be involved in education. Many parishes throughout the country purchase a copy of *It's Your Move!* for Year 6 children at their local primary school to support transition to secondary education. This splendid little book comes highly recommended. Other opportunities for individuals and parishes engaging with schools may be explored in the Scripture Union publication *Generation to Generation* and in the information paper *Individual and Parish Opportunities for Service and Contact with Schools*. To conclude, a final reflection for those Christians who are considering involvement in education, or indeed for those who are already engaged in education. There can be a parallel between Christian involvement in education and Jesus at the Last Supper when he '*took*', '*blessed*', '*broke*' and '*gave*'.

For those Christians who see involvement in education as a part of their Christian service, and indeed teaching as a vocation, there is a very real sense in which they have been *taken* by the Lord. In so doing they are commissioned for service and as such they are *blessed* for their unique work. In a similar way that the bread could not be given until it had been broken into pieces, so too in the education parallel, until we are *broken* of our preconceptions and prejudices we will not be able to truly *give*. A Christian vocation in education, at whatever level (teacher, governor, support staff, volunteer) will be painful at times, as we deal with the reality presented to us day by day. Yet by being there, supporting, encouraging and affirming, we are signs of Christian service and witness in the world.

BOOKS, ETC.

Individual and Parish Opportunities for Service and Contact with Schools, Sheffield Diocesan Board of Education (web address: www.sheffield.anglican.org)

It's Your Move (Bletchley: Scripture Union, 2000)

Radford, Sue *et al.*, *Generation to Generation: Building Bridges Between Church and Schools* (Scripture Union, 1999), available from Sheffield Diocesan Education Department

Schools – Building On Success, Green Paper (February 2001)

The Way Ahead: Church of England Schools in the New Millennium, Report of Lord Dearing's Church Schools Review Group (London: Church House Publishing, 2003)

Wood, Gillian, *Linking Churches and Schools* (London: Churches Together in England, 2003)

'Church Schools in the New Millennium', video produced by Blackburn Diocesan Board of

Education to help parishes, schools, deaneries and Parochial Church Councils explore the 1998 General Synod Resolution

'The Challenge of a Lifetime', video presenting *The Way Ahead*, commissioned by the Church of England's Board of Education and the National Society